PUFFI

Editor:

THE NEW NOAH

If you want to know how to capture, and then make friends with, an ant-eater, an electric eel, or a porcupine or a boa-constrictor, this is your book.

When Gerald Durrell goes wild-animal hunting he takes interest and affection along with his nets and traps. And his captives enjoy luxury treatment as he discovers how to feed and train them and prepare them for display in the zoos to which they are destined.

This is a fascinating book, for Mr Durrell lets you into many secrets of the animal hunter's trade as well as introducing you to a variety of charming and curious animals such as capybaras, hoatzins, and tucotucos, not to mention a tame curassow called Cuthbert.

There is an index for really enthusiastic naturalists, and the text is embellished with drawings by Ralph Thompson and photographs by Suschitzky.

For boys and girls with a taste for adventure.

Cover photographs by Jane Burton/Photo Researchers, and Paul Popper Ltd

GERALD DURRELL

The New Noah

With drawings by

RALPH THOMPSON

PENGUIN BOOKS

Penguin Books Ltd, Harmondsworth, Middlesex, England
Penguin Books Australia Ltd, Ringwood, Victoria, Australia

—

First published by Collins 1955
Published in Peacock Books 1962
Reprinted 1963
Reissued in Puffin Books 1966
Reprinted 1968, 1969

—

—

Made and printed in Great Britain
by Hazell Watson & Viney Ltd,
Aylesbury, Bucks
Set in Linotype Baskerville

This book is for my niece Sappho Jane
and my nephews Gerald Martin
and David Nicholas

CONTENTS

PART THREE

PERAMBULATIONS IN PARAGUAY

INTRODUCTION

MOST people at one time or another pay a visit to the zoological gardens. While there, they are so interested in the animals to be seen that they do not stop to wonder how a great many of them got to the zoo in the first place.

Now I am an animal collector and my job is to travel to the far-away places where these beasts live, and bring them back alive for the zoos. In this book I have described three animal-collecting trips that I have taken to various parts of the world, and have tried to show how the difficult but interesting job of collecting is done.

Most people have no idea of the hard work and worry that goes into a collecting trip to produce the fascinating birds and animals that they pay to see in the zoo. One of the questions that I am always asked is how I became an animal collector in the first place. The answer is that I have always been interested in animals and in zoos.

According to my parents, the first word I was able to say with any clarity was not the conventional 'Mamma' or 'Dadda', but the word 'Zoo', which I would repeat over and over again in a shrill voice until someone, in order to shut me up, would take me to the zoo. When I grew a little older, we lived in Greece and I had a great number of pets, ranging from owls to sea-horses, and I spent all my spare time exploring the countryside in search of fresh specimens to add to my collection of pets. Later on I went for a year to Whipsnade Zoo, as a student keeper, to get experience of the larger animals, such as lions, bears, bison, and ostrich, which were not so easy to keep at home. When I left, I luckily had enough money of my own to be able to finance my first trip and I have been going out regularly ever since then.

Though a collector's job is not an easy one and full of many disappointments, it is certainly a job which will appeal to all those who love animals and travel. In this book I have tried to show that the hard work and disappointments are nearly always more than offset by the thrill of your successes and the excitement and pleasure not only of capturing your animals but of seeing them alive in their natural haunts.

PART ONE

Collecting in the Cameroons

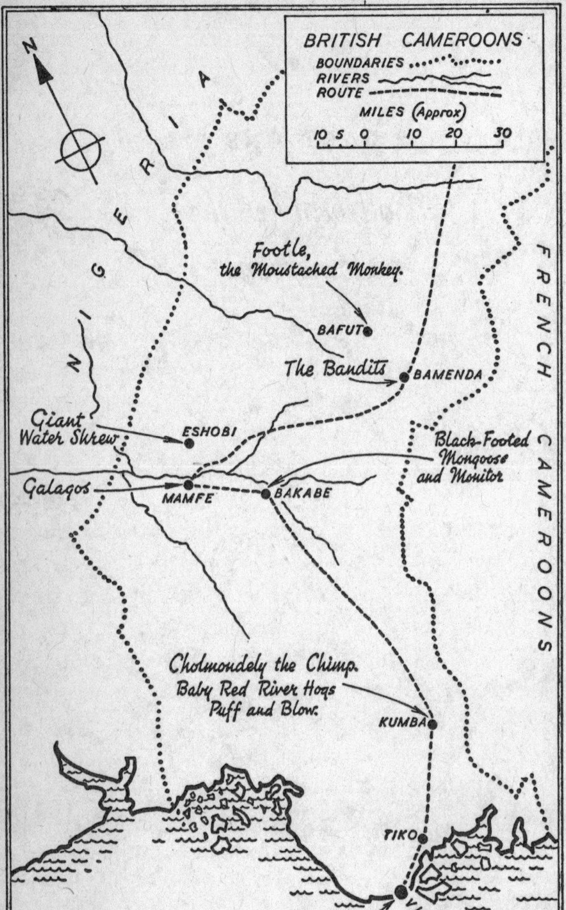

Since this book was first published the British Cameroons have been divided. The northern area is now part of Nigeria, and the southern part is united with the French Cameroons to form the Republic of Cameroun. The names in the text have not been altered, as they were correct when the book was written.

CHAPTER ONE

In which I have a tug-of-war with a Nile monitor

BEFORE starting out on a collecting trip you have to know what wild animals are wanted by the zoos; then, knowing their whereabouts, you choose those areas in which not only the specimens required are to be found, but other rare creatures as well. Zoologists and biologists, generally, have not the time or the money to travel to these distant corners of the earth to find out about wild life on the spot. Therefore, the animals have to be caught and brought back to them, so that they can be studied more conveniently in the zoo. Now, the larger and commoner creatures from most parts of the world are well represented in nearly all zoological collections, and quite a lot is known about them. So it was the smaller and rarer beasts, about which we know so little, that I wanted to collect. It is about them that I am going to write.

From many points of view it is sometimes the small animals in a country that influence man more than the large ones. At home, for instance, the brown rat does more damage every year than any of the larger creatures. It was for this reason that I concentrated during my collecting trips on the smaller forms of life. For my first expedition I chose the Cameroons, since it is a small, almost forgotten corner of Africa, which is more or less as it was before the advent of the white man. Here, in the gigantic rain forests, the animals live their lives as they have done for thousands of years.

It is of great value to get to know and study these wild creatures before they are influenced by civilization, for wild animals can be affected just as much by change as people. One of the results of cutting down forests, building towns, damming rivers, and driving roads through jungle, is an interference with their way of life, and they have either to adapt themselves to the new conditions or die out.

It was my intention to find out all I could about the animals of the great forests and to bring back as big and varied a collection as possible of its small fauna, the creatures that the African calls in pidgin English, 'small beef'.

When I arrived in the Cameroons for the first time what struck me most was the very vivid colouring of the undergrowth and the enormous size of the trees. There were leaves of every shade of green and red imaginable, from bottle green to pale jade, and from pink to crimson. The trees towered up to two and three hundred feet into the air, their trunks almost the circumference of a factory chimney, and their massive branches weighed down with leaves and flowers and great coiling creepers.

I landed at the little port of Victoria and had to spend a week or so there, preparing for the journey into the interior. A great many things had to be done before I could start on the actual work of collecting. There were Africans to engage as cooks or house-boys, various stores to buy and a great many other things as well. Also, the necessary permits to hunt and capture the animals I was after had to be obtained, for all the animal life in the Cameroons is strictly protected and, unless you obtain Government permission, you are not allowed to capture or kill any animals or birds. Eventually, when all this had been done, a lorry was hired and the food and equipment piled into it, and I set off. In those days there was only one way leading into the

interior of the Cameroons and this, if followed far enough, led you to the village of Mamfe on the banks of the Cross River, some 300 miles from the coast. It was at this village I had chosen to make my base camp.

The earth you find in the Cameroons is red, very like the earth you see in Devon, and so the road, winding through the hills, was a bright brick colour, lined on each side by immense forest trees. As we drove along, I could see hosts of brilliant birds feeding in the trees, tiny glittering sun-birds sipping nectar from the flowers, great glowing plantain-eaters, like giant magpies, eating wild figs; and sometimes the passage of the lorry would frighten a flock of hornbills which would fly off across the road, making tremendous swishing noises with their wings, and honking dismally.

In the short undergrowth at the side of the road scuttled large numbers of agama lizards. These reptiles are almost as bright in colour as the birds, for the males have vivid orange heads, and the body is decked out in blue, silver, red, and black, while the females are rose-coloured with bright apple-green spots. They have a curious habit of nodding their heads vigorously up and down, and look very peculiar dashing here and there in pursuit of each other, suddenly stopping to nod their brightly-coloured heads. Almost as numerous as these lizards were the pygmy kingfishers, minute little birds, smaller than a sparrow, with bright blue backs, orange shirt fronts, and coral red beaks and feet. Unlike the English kingfisher, these little birds live on locusts, grasshoppers, and other insects. Dozens of them were perched on the telegraph wires, or on the stumps of dead trees on the roadside, all peering down hopefully into the grass and bushes below. Occasionally, one of them would drop off his perch like a stone and, when he fluttered out of the grass again, a grasshopper that was almost the same size as himself would be clutched firmly in his beak.

Three days after leaving the coast I reached Mamfe. I had chosen this village as a base camp for a variety of reasons. When you are collecting wild animals you have to choose your base very carefully: it has to be within fairly easy reach of some sort of store, so that you can obtain sufficient supplies of tinned food, nails, wire netting, and other important things, and also it has to be fairly near a road, so that when the time comes to depart you can bring your lorries near enough to the camp to load up.

Secondly, you have to make sure that your base is going to be in a good collecting area, a place where there are not too many farms or people so that most of the wild animals have been driven away.

Mamfe was excellent in this respect, so a camp clearing was made on the banks of the river, about a mile away from the village, and the big marquee I had brought was erected. For the next six months this marquee was to act as a home for myself and my animals.

The first thing I had to do, before I could even start collecting, was to make sure that the base camp was functioning smoothly. Cages, pens, and ponds had to be built, as well as palm-thatched huts for the Africans I employed. I had to arrange for an adequate food and water supply, for when you have collected two or three hundred animals and birds, they manage to eat and drink a very great quantity every day. Another important thing was to interview as many of the local chiefs as possible, showing them drawings and photographs of the creatures I wanted, and telling them how much I was willing to pay for specimens. Then, when they went back to their villages, they told their people, and so eventually I had all the villagers for miles around helping me in my work.

Then, when everything was ready and there was a great pile of empty cages waiting to be filled, I could start hunting the strange animals that I had travelled so far to find.

There are really no set rules about capturing animals. It all depends on the type of country in which you are operating and the sort of animals you want to get hold of. There were several different methods that I used in the Cameroons, and one of the most successful was to hunt in the forest with the aid of native hunting dogs. These dogs wear little wooden bells round their necks, so that when they disappear into the thick undergrowth in pursuit of an animal you will know whereabouts they are and can follow them by the clonking noise these bells make.

One of the most exciting hunts of this sort occurred when I went up the mountain called N'da Ali, twenty-five miles from the base camp. I had been told by native hunters that on the upper slopes of this mountain there was found a rare animal which I particularly wanted, the black-footed mongoose, a very large mongoose, pure creamy-white in colour with chocolate-coloured legs and feet. I knew that a live specimen of this animal had never been seen in England, and so I was determined to try to capture one if I possibly could.

We set off on our hunt very early one morning, four hunters as well as myself, and a pack of five rather mangy-looking dogs. One of the drawbacks of this type of hunting is that you cannot explain to the dogs exactly what sort of animal it is you want to catch, and so they pick up the scent of any and every creature in the forest and follow it. The result is that while you might go out hunting for a mongoose, it is more likely that you will end up catching something completely different. As a matter of fact that is exactly what did happen.

We had been walking for about half an hour through the forest when the dogs picked up a fresh scent and rushed off yapping excitedly, with the sound of their bells echoing through the trees. We set off in hot pursuit, and for half an hour followed the distant sounds of the pack, running as hard as we could and feeling more and more exhausted. Suddenly, the leading hunter came to a stop and held up his hand. We stood there, panting for breath and straining our ears for the sound of the bells, but the forest around us was silent.

We spread out in a circle and walked through the trees in different directions, trying to find out which way the pack had gone. At last a shrill yodel from one of the hunters sent us all hurrying to the spot where he was waiting, and in the distance we could hear the sound of running water. As we ran towards it, the hunter explained to me, between gasps for breath, that, if the dogs had been led to the edge of the river by the quarry, the roaring of the water would cover up the noise of the bells. This explained how we had managed to lose the pack.

When we reached the water, we splashed our way upstream and came eventually to a place where the water cascaded and foamed over a small waterfall some twenty feet high. Round the base of the fall was a great jumbled mass of huge boulders fully overgrown with moss and small plants, and amongst these big rocks we could see the backs of the dogs, while above the roar of the water we could hear their shrill yapping. Peering among the rocks, we saw for the first time what it was we had been hunting: it was a tremendous Nile monitor, a great lizard, measuring six feet in length, with a long whip-like tail and heavy curved claws on his feet. He had backed himself into a cul-de-sac among the rocks and was facing the opening and keeping the pack at bay by lashing with his great tail and hissing with open mouth if they ventured too closely.

We were about to call the dogs off when one of them, more stupid than the rest, rushed in among the rocks and grabbed hold of the monitor's neck, hanging on as tightly as she could. The monitor returned the compliment by clasping her ear in his mouth, and then hunching himself up he brought his great hind legs on to the dog's back, ripping the skin open with his sharp claws. The dog, giving a yelp of pain, let go of his neck, and, as she started to retreat, the monitor lashed round with his tail and sent her rolling over and over among the rocks. Hastily we called the rest of the dogs off and tied them to a nearby tree, and then we had to decide on the best way to capture the lizard, who lay hissing among the rocks like some great prehistoric monster.

We tried to throw a net over him but the sharp-edged rocks kept getting caught in the folds, and in the end we gave this up as a bad job. The only other method I could think of was to climb up above him and, while someone attracted his attention, get a noose round his neck. Explaining to the hunters what I wanted done, I scrambled up over the slippery rocks until I was perched about six feet above the place where the monitor lay. I made a running noose at the end of a long piece of rope and then, leaning over, lowered it gently towards the reptile. He did not appear to associate the length of rope with the human beings about him, and so it was quite easy for me to work the noose over his head and pull it back gently until it lay round his neck. Then I pulled it tight.

Unfortunately, in my excitement, I had forgotten to

tie the end of the rope to anything and, what is more, I was kneeling on the loose end. As soon as the monitor felt the noose tighten round his neck, he shot forward like a rocket, pulling the rope taut, so that it jerked my knees from under me and I started to slip over the edge of the rock. On that smooth surface, wet with spray from the waterfall, I could find nothing to grip, and so I slipped over the edge and crashed down into the gully below. As I fell, I remember hoping that the

monitor would be so frightened by my sudden appearance out of the clouds that he would not wait to give battle. I had no desire to get any closer than necessary to his well-armed feet. Luckily, that is exactly what happened. The monitor was so startled that he dashed out from among the rocks and scuttled off down the river bank, trailing the rope behind him. But he did not get very far, for as soon as he was clear of the rocks, the natives threw the net over him and within a few seconds he was writhing and hissing in its folds. We eventually got him out of the net and tied to a long pole, and I dispatched one of the hunters back to camp with him.

I was extremely pleased to have caught this big reptile, but it was not exactly what we had come up the mountain to hunt for, and so we continued on our way through the forest.

It was not long before the dogs picked up a fresh scent. The chase they led us on this time was a far longer one and much more interesting than our chase after the monitor had been. First of all, the animal we were hunting ran downhill and we had to run desperately down the slope, leaping and jumping over fallen rocks, which was really rather dangerous, as a slip could have meant a broken leg or something even worse. Then our quarry turned round and ran uphill again, and we were forced to follow, with our hearts pounding and with sweat streaming off us.

This hunt lasted for three-quarters of an hour and eventually, following the sound of the dog bells, we came to a level area of forest where we found the pack grouped round one end of a great hollow tree trunk that lay across the forest floor. Sitting in the mouth of the hollow trunk was a big white animal with a curiously bear-like face and small ears. He was staring with an expression of great scorn on his face at the dogs that were yapping and snarling around him. One of the dogs, I noticed, had a bite on his nose, and so I understood why they were keeping such a discreet distance from this strange animal. When the black-footed mongoose saw us, he turned round and disappeared into the hollow interior of the tree.

We called the pack off and placed a net over the end of the trunk and then went up to the other end to make sure there was no exit hole. There was none, and so we knew that the mongoose had only one way of getting out of the trunk, and that was guarded by our net. The only thing now was to get him out of the tree. Luckily, the wood was very rotten and soft, and so by cutting with our knives we managed to make a hole at the opposite end of the trunk to where the net had been hung. We then laid a small fire inside the hole, and when it was nicely alight we piled green leaves on top of it, so a thick pungent smoke rushed down the hollow tree. For some time we could hear the mongoose inside coughing in an irritated manner, but finally the smoke became too much for him and he shot out of the end of the trunk and into the net where he rolled over and over, snapping and snarling. After a certain amount of difficulty, during which we were nearly all bitten, we managed to get him out of the net and into a strong bag. Then we carried him triumphantly back to camp.

For the first two or three days he was very savage and would attack the bars of the cage whenever I went near. But after a while in captivity he grew quite tame and within two or three weeks would even come and take food from my hand, or let me scratch him behind his ears.

In the mountains of the Cameroons the thick forest gives way to rolling mountain grassland, and in this sort of country I had to use other methods of capturing animals, one of the best of which was to drive the creatures into nets.

It was to this grassland territory that I went to capture the giant booming squirrel, the biggest squirrel found in the Cameroons, an animal about twice the size of the ordinary English grey squirrel. These squirrels are found also in the lowlands, but there they spend their time in the top branches of the very tallest trees, feeding on the fruit and nuts that grow up there, and very rarely coming down to the ground. This makes it almost impossible to catch them. In the grasslands, however, they live in the small strips of forests that border the stream and in the early morning and evening they would come down and venture out into the grass fields in search of food. My hunters had told me they knew of a section of forest land where these squirrels were plentiful, and I decided that we would try to catch them in the early morning when they came down into the grass to feed.

We set off about one o'clock in the morning and arrived at the place just before dawn. A suitable spot was chosen in the grass at the edge of the forest and there we spread our nets in a half-moon, camouflaging them with grass and bushes. We had to do this while it was dark, and we had to be very quiet about it, so that the squirrels would not know we were there. Then, the nets being ready, we went and hid under some large bushes at the very edge of the strip of forest and waited there, drenched with dew, until the dawn broke. In the mountains the climate is much colder than in the lowlands, and so by the time the sun rose we were frozen and our teeth were chattering with cold.

Presently, as the morning mist swirled about us in great white clouds, we heard some loud angry 'chuck-chuck' noises echoing from the trees around us, and the hunters whispered that this meant the squirrels were preparing to come down for their breakfast. Soon, peering through the leaves towards the part of the grass fields where our nets were concealed, I saw a strange object bobbing up and down. It looked exactly like a long black and white balloon, and I could not for the life of me think what it could be. I pointed it out to the hunters and they explained that it was a squirrel's tail bobbing up and down above the grass stalks while its body was hidden from view. Very soon this solitary 'balloon' was joined by several others, and as the mist rose we could see the squirrels themselves hopping cautiously from tussock to tussock, sitting up on their great black and white striped tails.

When we judged that they were far enough away from the trees, we rose from our cramped positions and spread out in a line. Then I gave the signal and we all walked slowly out into the grass field. Our appearance was greeted with a chorus of loud frightened chucking noises from the squirrels in the trees behind us. The ones in the grass field, however, just sat and stared at us suspiciously. Our plans to walk forward, driving the squirrels farther and farther away from the trees and slowly to the nets, and then, once they were within the circle of the nets, suddenly to charge down and stampede them, so that in their panic they would run into the mesh before they saw us, did not, however, work out quite the way we expected.

One of the squirrels, more cunning than the rest, suddenly realized that we were driving him away from the sanctuary of the tall trees, and so he broke away to the left, skirted round the line of hunters and raced back into the forest. The other squirrels sat and watched, obviously undecided as to whether or not they should follow him. They were not quite within the circle of the nets, but I felt that if we did not charge them they would all break away and get round us as the first squirrel had done. So we all charged forward, shouting and yelling and waving our arms, trying to appear as frightening as possible. The squirrels took one look at us and turned and fled.

Two of them broke away to the left and right, and three others ran straight into the net and within a few seconds were struggling helplessly in the mesh. It was an extremely difficult job to disentangle them, for they uttered loud snarling grunts of rage and bit savagely at our hands with their orange-coloured teeth. They were quite handsome animals, with russet-red upper parts, lemon-yellow bellies, and the big black and white ringed tails, each of which measured about eighteen inches in length. Now that the squirrels in the forest knew we were trying to catch them, it was useless to go on with the hunt, and so we had to be content with the three that we had captured.

We carried them back to camp in thick canvas bags and placed them in a nice roomy cage with a good supply of fruit and vegetables, and left them to settle down. After they had thoroughly explored the cage, they ate up all the food that I had put in it and then curled up and went to sleep.

It was very early the next morning when I discovered how these squirrels had come by their name. I was woken up at dawn by a very strange noise coming from the cage, and on creeping from my bed I could see the squirrels sitting near the wire front of their cage and giving their weird cry. It started off as a gentle thrumming sound, such as you hear in a telegraph pole when the wind is shaking the wires. It gradually grew louder and louder and more metallic until it sounded exactly like the dying noise of a huge gong being struck. The squirrels produced this extraordinary sound every morning at dawn and thereafter for the first week, until I grew used to it, I was always woken up at that unearthly hour, which made me begin to think that it was rather a doubtful privilege to have captured these animals.

CHAPTER TWO

In which I become involved with baby crocodiles, bush-tailed porcupines, and various snakes

---

WHEN, as a result of hunting every day, I had managed to collect a lot of animals, I began to find that I had less and less time to go out into the forest, for my captives required a great deal of attention. There was, consequently, only one course left, and that was to go hunting at night. It was perhaps one of the most exciting ways of searching.

Armed with very bright torches and the usual collection of bags, bottles, boxes, and nets, the hunters and I would set off shortly after dark and walk quietly among the huge trees, shining our torches into the branches above. If any animals were there, you could see their eyes glowing in the torch beam, like strange jewels among the leaves.

This is really a very good method of hunting, for in this way you come across a lot of creatures which you never see during the daytime, since all the nocturnal ones that spend the daylight hours sleeping in their dens come out to feed and hunt during the night. Once you have located them in the tree-tops, or on the ground, you then have the job of trying to catch your quarry, and this is generally no easy matter.

Strangely enough, one of the easiest creatures to obtain in this way is the baby crocodile. These reptiles live in small, shallow streams which criss-cross through the forest, and at night come out on to the miniature sandbanks and lie there, waiting hopefully in case some small creature should come down to drink there, and they could catch it.

We used to follow the courses of the streams, wading sometimes waist-deep in the water, shining our torches ahead of us. Quite suddenly, on a sandbank, there would appear what looked like two red-hot coals gleaming in my torch beam, and, keeping the light steady, I would approach cautiously and, eventually, see the baby crocodile lying on the sand, his head raised suspiciously, glaring at me. I would direct the torch beam carefully into his eyes, so that he would be dazzled by its light and not notice me behind it. Then I would edge close enough to lean forward and pin him down by the back of his neck with the aid of a forked stick.

Most of these beasts were only about eighteen inches or two feet long, but occasionally I found some that were a bit bigger, being four feet or more in length. They would put up quite a struggle when I pinned them down with this forked stick, lashing out with their tails and trying to get back into the water, uttering deep rumbling roars, rather as though they were lions instead of crocodiles.

When picking up a crocodile, I not only had to watch his mouth, but his tail as well, for a big one has so much strength in his tail that a whipping blow from it could quite easily break your arm. Another trick they had was lying quite still and allowing me to pick them up by the back of the neck; then, without warning, they would give a terrific wriggle and slap me furiously with their tails, and this sudden movement would be so unexpected that my hold would be broken and I would drop the crocodile back into the water. So we made it a rule never to pick up a crocodile unless we had a firm grip on the back of the neck and on the tail.

One of the most difficult and painful night hunts I had, occurred when I was staying at a small village called Esholi.

We had been hunting nearly the whole night without very much luck, when one of the hunters suggested that we make our way to a certain place of which he knew, where there was a cliff with a great number of caves in it. Here, we thought we should be able to find some sort of creature.

We set off and came eventually to a wide river which we had to cross. We waded through the cold water, waist-deep, and when we were in the middle, the hunter behind me switched on his torch, and there all around us were dozens of water snakes, swimming to and fro, watching us with their bright eyes, their necks sticking out of the water like submarine periscopes. These snakes are not poisonous, although they can give a bite when they get angry. However, the Africans are convinced that every kind of snake is poisonous, and so they treat them all with great caution. My hunter, when he saw that he was stuck in the middle of a river surrounded on all sides by what seemed to be the entire water-snake population of the Cameroons, uttered loud yelps of fright and tried to run to the bank. Trying to run in water that is waist deep is not very easy and the current caught him off balance and he fell back into the water with a splash, dropping all the equipment that he had been carrying on his head.

The water snakes, frightened by this sudden commotion, all dived for cover.

When the hunter rose again, spluttering and gasping, and his companions asked him what was the matter, he said that the river was full of snakes, whereupon they switched on their torches and shone them on the surface of the water, but not a single water snake was to be seen. After a bit of an argument, I managed to persuade them all to stand still in the middle of the river and we switched off our torches and waited quietly for half an hour or so. When we all switched on our lights again, there were the water snakes once more, weaving silvery patterns in the water around us. With the aid of our long-handled butterfly nets, we succeeded in catching four or five of these snakes and dropping them wriggling and squirming into our collecting bags. Then we went on our way.

We reached the cliffs at last and found they were literally honeycombed with caves of all different shapes and sizes, the entrances of which were almost hidden by great masses of boulders and short undergrowth. We each took a section of the cliff and set to work to see what we could find.

As I was pushing along through the rocks, shining my torch hopefully here and there, I saw a peculiar shape jump out of a bush, scuttle across the ground and then dive into a small hole in the cliff face. I hurried forward, and kneeling down by the mouth of the cave, shone my torch up it, but there was nothing to be seen. The passage was about as wide as a door, but only some two feet high, and in order to get inside to where the animal had gone, I had to lie flat on my tummy, hold the torch in my mouth and pull myself slowly along. This was extremely uncomfortable, as the floor of the passage was sprinkled with sharp-edged rocks of various shapes, and so my progress was slow and painful.

I found that this tunnel ended in a small circular room from which another led off, still deeper into the interior of the cliff. Crawling through this second passage I shone my torch down and discovered that it, too, ended in a little room, only far smaller than the one in which I was lying. As I was flashing my torch around, I heard two thumps, followed by a crisp rustling sound, rather like a rattle. Before I could see what had produced this noise, there was another burst of rattling and something hurled itself out of the gloom of the cave, knocked the torch out of my hand, and ran what felt like fifty needles into my wrist. I retrieved the torch and retreated hastily to examine my wrist which was scratched and pricked as though I had plunged it into a blackberry bush.

Crawling back up the tunnel again I shone the torch round and the beam picked out the animal which had attacked me. It was a fully-grown bush-tailed porcupine. These curious-looking animals, the hindquarters of which are covered with long, sharp quills, have a naked tail which ends in a bunch of prickles, rather like an ear of wheat. By shaking this bunch of quills on the end of their tails, they produce a strange rattling noise, which was the sound I had heard.

The porcupine had turned his back on me and erected all his quills and was peering over his shoulder with bulging and indignant eyes and stamping his feet warningly. I decided that the only part of his anatomy I could grasp without much risk of being pricked by his spikes was his tail. So I wrapped my hand in a thick canvas bag, reached forward, and grabbed him just below the tuft of spikes on his tail. The first thing he did was to run backwards, crushing my hand against the rocks, his spikes going through the canvas bag like a knife through butter. However, I hung on and tried to pull him out and push him into another bag which I held in my other hand. I was so cramped in that narrow passage that it was impossible to manoeuvre the bag successfully over the porcupine's

head, and every movement he made seemed to jab yet another of his quills into me. It ended up by him backing into my chest, and, as I was only wearing a thin shirt, this was very painful, to say the least.

I decided that the best thing to do was to try to pull the porcupine outside the cave before endeavouring to get him into the bag, and so, taking a firmer grip on his tail, I proceeded to crawl backwards, slowly and carefully, pulling the reluctant porcupine after me. It seemed to take hours before I eventually reappeared in the open air and all the fight seemed to go out of him, for he dangled there quite limply. I shouted for the hunters and when they joined me we succeeded in getting him into a bag. I was scratched and bruised from head to foot and felt that the porcupine had made me pay very dearly for his capture.

There were, of course, many other methods which we employed in collecting our specimens. We set great numbers of traps, for example, in different parts of the forest, but this had to be very carefully done, for most of the forest animals have their own particular area in which they live, and they seldom venture outside this territory. They follow certain paths, both on the ground and in the tree-tops, and so, unless your trap has been set in exactly the right place, it is more than likely that the creature will never come anywhere near it. Most people think that in the great forests the animals wander far and wide all the time, but this is not so. Each picks the territory that suits it best and sticks to it, and sometimes these areas are large, but more often than not they are amazingly small, and in a lot of instances an animal inhabits a patch of ground which is very little bigger than a large cage in a zoo. Provided that an animal can find a good supply of food and water, and a safe place to sleep, within a limited area, he will not venture out of it.

A lot of people seem to think that catching wild animals is a very dangerous task, but that to go off into the forest at night in search of specimens is nothing short of madness. Actually, the depths of the forests are not dangerous, and they are no more dangerous by night than they are by day. You will find that all wild animals are only too eager to get out of your way when they hear you coming. Only if you have them cornered will they attack you, and you can hardly blame them for that. But in the forest you will find that all the creatures which live there (and this includes snakes) are very well behaved and only want to be left alone. If you don't harm them they most certainly are not going to go out of their way to try to hurt you.

So, collecting wild animals is not as dangerous as some people imagine. Generally, it is only as dangerous as your own stupidity allows it to be: in other words, if you take silly risks you must expect unpleasant consequences. Sometimes, of course, in the heat of the moment, you take a risk without realizing it, and it is only afterwards that you find out how stupid you were.

On my second trip to West Africa I met a young man on board the ship, going out there to take up a job on a banana plantation. He confessed to me that the only thing he was really afraid of was snakes. I told him that snakes were, as a rule, only too anxious to get out of the way, and in any case, they were few and far between, and it was unlikely that he would see many of them. He appeared greatly encouraged by this information, and promised that while I was up country he would try to get some specimens for me. I thanked him, and forgot all about it.

When I had made my collection, I travelled down to the coast with it to board the ship. The night before we sailed, my young friend turned up in his car, very excited, to tell me that he had got the specimens he had promised. He said that on the banana plantation where he worked he had discovered a pit which was full of snakes, and they were all mine, provided I went and got them out!

Without bothering to inquire what this pit was like, I agreed, and we set off in his car to the plantation. On arrival at his bungalow I found that my friend had invited several other people to watch my snake hunt. Then, while we were having a drink, I noticed that my friend was searching round for something, and when I asked him what he was looking for he told me it was some rope. I asked him what he wanted the rope for, and he explained that it was to lower me into the pit with. This made me inquire for the first time what sort of pit it was, for I had imagined something about thirty feet square and about three feet deep.

I discovered to my dismay that the pit resembled a large grave, being about twelve feet long, about three feet wide and some ten feet deep. My friend had decided that the only way for me to get down there was to lower me on the end of a rope, like a pantomime fairy! I hastily explained that in order to catch snakes in a pit like that I would have to have a torch, which I had not got. None of the other members of the party had a torch either, but my friend solved the problem.

He tied the big paraffin pressure lamp on to the end of a long string, and explained that he would lower this into the pit with me. I could not protest, for, as my friend rightly pointed out, it gave a much better light than any torch. Then we all walked out through the moonlit banana plantation towards the pit, and I remember thinking to myself on the way that there was just a chance the snakes might turn out to be a harmless variety. But when we reached the edge of the pit and lowered the light into it I saw that it was full of baby Gaboon vipers, perhaps one of the most deadly snakes in West Africa, and all of them seemed very annoyed at being disturbed, and lifted their spade-shaped heads and hissed at us.

Now I had not thought that I would have to go down into the pit with the snakes in order to catch them, and so I was wearing the wrong sort of clothes. Thin trousers and a pair of Plimsoll shoes are no protection at all against the inch-long fangs of a Gaboon viper. I explained this to my friend, and he very kindly lent me *his* trousers and shoes, which were quite thick and strong. So, as I could think of no more ex-

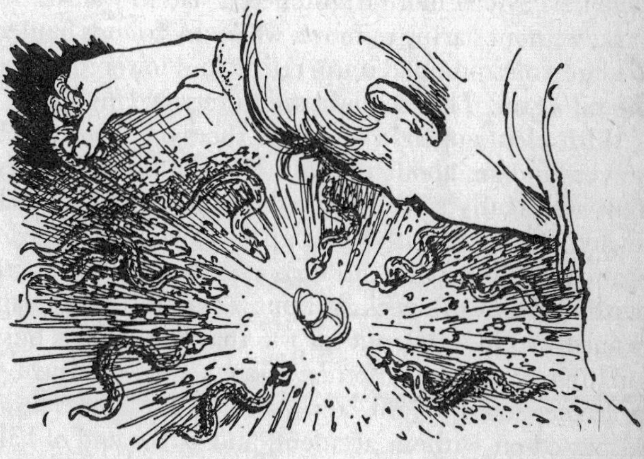

cuses, they tied the rope round my waist and started to lower me into the pit.

I very soon discovered that the rope had been fastened round my waist with a slip-knot, and the lower I got into the pit the tighter grew the slip-knot round my waist, until I could hardly breathe.

Just before I landed at the bottom I called up and told my friends to stop lowering me: I wanted to examine the ground that I was going to land on, to make sure there were no snakes in the way. The area being clear, I shouted to them to lower away, and at that moment two things happened.

First, the light, which no one had remembered to pump up in the excitement, went out; secondly, one of the shoes which I had borrowed off my friend, and which were too large for me, came off. So there was I, standing at the bottom of a ten-foot deep pit, with no light and no shoe on one foot, surrounded by seven or eight deadly and extremely irritated Gaboon vipers. I have never been more frightened. I had to wait in the dark, without daring to move, while my friends hauled the lamp out, pumped it up, relit it and lowered it into the pit again. Then I could see to retrieve my shoe.

With plenty of light and both shoes on, I felt much braver, and set about the task of catching the vipers. This was really simple enough. I had a forked stick in my hand, and with this I approached each reptile, pinned it down with the fork and then picked it up by the back of the neck and put it into my snake bag. What I had to watch out for was that while I was busy catching one snake, another might wriggle round behind me and I might step back on it. However, it all passed off without accident, and at the end of half an hour I had caught eight of the baby Gaboon vipers.

I thought that was quite enough to be going on with, and so my friends hauled me out of the pit. I decided, after that night, that collecting was only as dangerous as your own stupidity allowed it to be, no more and no less.

CHAPTER THREE

In which Puff and Blow take over

WHEN the base camp was finished, it looked rather as though a circus had moved into the forest, and it looked even more like a circus when the camp had started filling up with specimens we had captured. Along one side of the marquee was a line of cages in which I kept all the smaller animals, a great variety of creatures that ranged from mice to mongooses.

The first cage in the row belonged to a couple of baby red river hogs which I had called Puff and Blow, and they were the most charming pair of babies imaginable. A full-grown red river hog is about the most colourful and handsome of the pig family. Its fur is a rich orange-red colour and along its back and neck is a mane of pure white fur; on the tips of its long, pointed ears are two dangling tufts of white hair. Puff and Blow, however, like all baby piglets, were striped; they were a dark chocolate brown, and their stripes were a light buttercup yellow, running from nose to tail. This made them look like fat little wasps, as they trotted round their pen.

Puff was the first one to arrive at the camp. He was brought in one morning, sitting rather sadly in a wicker basket balanced on the head of a native hunter. He had been captured in the forest, and I soon discovered the reason for his doleful appearance was that he had eaten nothing for two days, a thing that was enough to make any self-respecting pig look down in the snout. The hunter who had caught him had tried to feed him on bananas but Puff was far too young for that sort of food. What he wanted was milk, and plenty of it. So, as soon as I had paid for him, I mixed a big bottleful of warm milk with sugar, and taking Puff on to my knees, I tried to make him drink. He was about the size of a pekinese, with very small hooves and a pair of sharp little tusks as well, as I soon found out to my cost.

Of course, he had never seen a feeding bottle before, and treated it with the gravest suspicion from the start. When I lifted him on to my knees and tried to put the rubber into his mouth, he decided that this was some special kind of torture I had invented for him. He screamed and squealed, kicking me with his sharp little hooves and trying to stab me with his little tusks. After the struggle between us had lasted for about five minutes, both Puff and I looked as though we had been bathed in milk, but not a single drop of it had gone down his throat.

I filled another bottle and again grasped the squealing pig firmly between my knees, wedged his mouth open with one hand, and started to squirt the milk in with the other. He was so busily squeaking for help that every time the milk was squirted into his mouth, the next squeal would spit it all out again. At last I was fortunate enough to get a few drops to trickle down his throat, and waited for him to get the taste of it, which he soon made apparent by stopping to yell and struggle, and by starting to smack his lips and grunt. I dribbled a little more milk into his mouth and he sucked it down greedily, and within a short while he was pulling away at the bottle as though he would never stop, while his tummy grew bigger and bigger. At length, when the last drop had disappeared from the bottle, he heaved a long sigh of satisfaction and fell into a deep sleep on my lap, snoring like a hive full of bees.

After that he was no more trouble, and after a few days had lost all his fear of humans, and would run, grunting and squeaking delightedly, to the bars of his pen when he saw me coming, and flop over on his back to have his tummy scratched. At feeding time, when he saw the bottle coming, he would push his nose through the bars and scream shrilly with excitement, and, to hear him, you would think he had never had a square meal in his life.

After Puff had been with me for about two weeks, Blow arrived on the scene. She had also been caught in the forest by a native hunter and had objected to it most strongly. Long before she, or her captor, had appeared in sight, I could hear her loud squealing protest, and she never stopped once until I had bought her and put her into the cage next to Puff's. I did not house them together straight away, for she was a bit bigger than Puff, and I thought she might hurt him.

As soon as he saw there was another pig like himself in the next cage he hurled himself at the bars between, grunting and squeaking with delight, and when Blow saw him, she stopped screaming and went over to investigate. They were as pleased to see each other as though they had been brother and sister. They rubbed noses through the bars between them, and since they seemed so friendly I decided to put them together straight away. In doing this I seemed justified, for they both ran forward and sniffed round each other excitedly: Puff gave a loud grunt and prodded Blow in the ribs with his nose; Blow grunted in return and skipped off across the cage. Then the fun started, round and round the cage Puff chased Blow; they ran, dodging and doubling, twisting and turning until both of them were quite exhausted and fell asleep on their bed of dry banana leaves, snoring and snoring until the whole cage vibrated.

Blow soon learnt to drink from the bottle like Puff, but, as she was a few weeks older, her diet included some solid food as well. So every day, after they had both had their bottles, I would put a flat pan full of soft fruit and vegetables into the cage and Blow would spend the morning with her nose stuck in this, squelching and snuffling about, dreamily, in true piggy fashion.

Puff did not like this at all. He was too young to eat solid food himself but did not see why Blow should do so if he could not. He felt that he was being done out of something, and would stand and watch her, as she ate, with an angry expression on his face, grunting to himself peevishly.

Sometimes he would try to drive her away from the food by pushing her with his head, and then Blow would wake up out of her dream among the mashed bananas and chase him angrily across the cage, squealing furiously. The longer Blow spent at her food dish, the more depressed Puff became.

The idea must have come to him one day that he too could get an extra meal by the simple method of sucking Blow's tail. I suppose her tail looked to him not unlike the end of the bottle from which he got his meal; anyway, he became convinced that if he sucked it long enough he would get an extra supply of delicious milk from it.

So there Blow would stand, grunting to herself, her nose buried in the soft fruit, while behind her Puff would be solemnly sucking her tail. She did not mind this as long as he only sucked; occasionally, however, he would become annoyed and impatient because no milk appeared, and would start to tug and bite with his sharp, little tusks. Then Blow would whisk round and chase him into the corner, pushing him hard in the ribs, and return muttering angrily to her delicious plate of food.

In the end, however, I was forced to separate them, only putting them together again for a game once a day, for Puff had sucked at Blow's tail so enthusiastically that he had removed all the hair and it had become quite bald. So for some time they lived next door to one another while Blow's tail grew new fur, and while Puff learnt to eat solid food.

Blow, for some unknown reason, was much more nervous than Puff, and as soon as he discovered this he used to go out of his way to frighten her. He would hide behind the fence and jump out on her when she passed, or else he would lie there pretending to be asleep, and as soon as Blow came near him would leap to his feet and charge her with loud grunts. One day he frightened her so much that she fell into the food and came out with bits of banana and mango stuck all over her.

Puff invented one special trick which he took great delight in playing on her every morning after their cage had been cleaned out. I would leave a pile of crisp, dry banana leaves in one corner for their bed; no sooner had I put it in, than Puff would race over, burrow down under the leaves until he was completely hidden, and wait there patiently, sometimes for as long as half an hour, until Blow came to see where he had gone. Then, with a loud squeal, he would leap out of the leaves and chase her across the pen. Sometimes, he would play this trick three times in a morning, but poor Blow would never learn from experience. As soon as he shot out of the leaves like a striped rocket, she would turn tail and run as fast as her fat legs would carry her, obviously thinking that it was

a leopard or something of a similar nature that was attacking her.

Since they spent most of their day chasing each other about or playing tricks on one another, the baby pigs naturally became very tired, and towards evening they would only just have enough energy left to eat their supper.

Sometimes, in fact, they would go to sleep while still sucking at the bottle and I would have to wake them up so that they could finish their meal. Then, grunting sleepily, they would burrow deep down into their bed of banana leaves and lie there side by side, snoring in chorus all through the night.

Just about the time that the baby pigs were going sleepily to bed, the animals in the cage next door were starting to wake up and take an interest in life. They were the galagos, or bush babies, tiny animals, the size of a newly-born kitten, which look rather like a cross between an owl and a squirrel with a bit of monkey thrown in. They had thick, soft, grey fur and long bushy tails. Their hands and feet were like a monkey's and they had enormous great golden eyes similar to an owl's.

All day the galagos would sleep curled up together in their bedroom, but towards evening, just as the sun was getting low, they would wake up and peer out of their bedroom door, yawning sleepily and blinking at you with their great astonished-looking eyes. Very slowly, they would come out into the cage, still yawning and stretching, and then the three of them would sit in a circle and have a wash and brush up.

This was a very lengthy and complicated performance. They would start with the very tips of their tails and slowly work upwards until every scrap of their furs had been combed and smoothed by their long, bony fingers; then, blinking their golden eyes at each other in self-satisfaction, they would begin the next job of the evening. This was doing their exercises. Sitting on their hind legs, they would stretch up as far as they could and suddenly jump up into the air, twisting right round to land facing in the opposite direction. After limbering up, they would start to leap and jump among the branches in their cage, ending up by chasing each other round and pulling one another's tails, until they had worked up an appetite for their supper. Then down they would come and sit by the door of the cage, staring out hopefully, waiting for me to appear with their food.

Their main course was finely chopped fruit with a dishful of sweetened milk. As a dessert, I would fetch a large tin in which was kept a delicacy that the

galagos liked best of all – grasshoppers. They would sit by the door, squeaking to each other, their long fingers trembling with excitement, watching me as I scooped out a handful of kicking grasshoppers. Opening the cage door, throwing in the insects and slamming the door shut had to be done in a matter of seconds.

Uproar would break out immediately in the cage: the grasshoppers leaped and jumped in all directions, and the galagos, their eyes almost popping out of their heads with excitement, would give chase, dashing madly round the cage, grabbing the grasshoppers and stuffing them into their mouths. As soon as their mouths were full, they would grab as many as they could in their hands, and then settle down to eat them as fast as possible, gobbling and grunting.

All the time they would watch with their big eyes, to see where the other grasshoppers were going, and to make quite sure that their companions did not have more than their fair share. As soon as the last succulent morsel had been gulped down, off they would go again in a mad chase after the remaining insects. Within a short while there would not be a single grasshopper left in the cage and only a few odd legs and wings would be lying scattered on the floor. The galagos, however, were never convinced of this, so they would spend an exciting hour examining every crack and crevice in the cage, in the hope that one of these delicacies would somehow be overlooked.

Each evening, as the sun was setting, I would clean out the galagos' cage and replace the dirty grass with a big handful of clean leaves. The galagos loved having a big bundle of foliage in the bottom of the cage, for they would play among the stalks and spend a lot of time searching for imaginary insects which they felt sure were hiding there.

One evening, I put grass in, as usual, and, quite by accident, put in with it a long stalk with a golden flower on the end, which looked very like a marigold. Some time later I passed the cage and was astonished to see one of the galagos sitting up on his hind legs with the flower clutched in one hand, slowly biting off the petals and eating them. The fluffy centre part of the flower he threw away, and one of his companions immediately seized this and began to play with it. First he tossed it up into the air and then chased it and 'killed' it in the corner, as he would do with a grasshopper. He did this so realistically that one of his companions must have thought he had a grasshopper, and went over to find out. The first galago ran off with the flower head in his mouth and the other two gave chase, all of them ending up by falling in a struggling heap on the bottom of the cage. By the time they had finished with it, the flower head was torn up into tiny pieces and scattered all over the place. They seemed to enjoy playing with this flower so much that every night afterwards I would put two or three of these marigolds into their cage and they would eat the petals and play 'catch-as-catch-can' with the remains.

Although I watched the galagos playing in their cage every evening and marvelled at their speed and graceful movements, I never realized quite how fast they could be until the night that one of them escaped.

They had finished their food, and I was removing the empty plates from the cage, when one of the little animals suddenly ran through the door, up my arms and jumped from my shoulder on to the roof of the cage. I made a grab at the end of his tail, but he bounded away like a rubber ball and perched on the very edge of the cage top, watching me. I moved round slowly and carefully, and made a quick grab at him, but long before my hand was anywhere near him he had launched himself into space. He jumped across a gap of about eight feet and landed as lightly as a feather on one of the centre poles of the marquee, clinging there as though he had been glued on. I dashed after him and he let me come quite close before moving. Then, without warning, he jumped off the pole, landed on my shoulder and immediately bounced off again on to the top of another cage. I chased him for about half an hour, and the hotter and more annoyed I became, the more he seemed to enjoy the whole business.

When I did catch him, it was quite by accident. He had jumped off a pile of old boxes on to the mosquito net over my camp bed, obviously thinking that the net was a firm surface to land on. Of course, his weight made the net sag and the next minute he was all tangled up in its folds. Before he could wriggle free, I had managed to rush forward and grab him. After that experience, I was very careful about opening the galagos' door.

CHAPTER FOUR

In which I am bitten by bandits

ANYONE passing the cage next door to the galagos', hearing the fearsome noises that came from its interior would have been excused for thinking that there was a pair of tigers locked in it; or, if not tigers, some equally fierce and noisy animal. Snarls, squeaks, screeches, and grunts combined with snuffles and growls could almost always be heard coming from inside this cage. All this uproar was made by three little animals a bit smaller than the average guinea-pig, which I had christened 'the bandits'. They were, in fact, baby kusimanses, a small animal like a mongoose, and for their size, they were far more nuisance than nearly all the other animals put together.

When they first arrived, they were each about the size of a small rat, and they had only just got their eyes open. Their fur was a bright gingery colour, sticking up in tufts and spikes all over their bodies, and they had long, pink, indiarubber noses that wiffled this way and that with curiosity.

At first, I had to feed them on milk and this was no easy job, for they drank more milk than any other baby animal I had ever seen; the whole business was made more difficult by the fact that they were far too small to be able to drink from the feeding bottle I used for the other baby animals. I had to feed them by wrapping a lump of cotton-wool round the end of a stick, dipping it in milk, and then letting them suck it.

This worked very well in the beginning, because they had no teeth, but as soon as their teeth appeared through the gums they began to be troublesome. They were so greedy that they would take hold of the cotton-wool and hang on to it like bulldogs, refusing to let go to allow me to dip it into the milk again. On many occasions, they bit so hard that the cotton-wool came off the end of the stick and they would then try to

swallow it. Only by putting my finger down their throats and capturing the wool as it was disappearing could I save them from being choked to death. They did not like having a finger stuck down their throats, as it always made them sick; and, of course, as soon as they had been sick, they would begin to feel hungry again and so we would have to repeat the whole performance.

As soon as they got their sharp little teeth, they began to feel very brave and venturesome, and they were always only too ready to poke their long noses into somebody else's business. I kept them at first in a basket near my bed so that I could feed them more easily during the night. The top for this basket was not too secure and the bandits were always climbing out and trotting off on tours of inspection around the camp. This worried me, because we had a number of dangerous animals there and the bandits seemed to have no fear, for they would stick their noses into a monkey's cage or a snake's box with equal freedom. They spent their lives in an endless search for food, and everything they came across they would bite, in the hopes that it would turn out to be something tasty.

On one occasion they had escaped from their basket, without my noticing, and had wandered round by the long line of monkey cages to see if they could find anything nice to eat. I had a monkey at that time with a very long, silky tail of which she was extremely proud. She used to spend hours every day grooming it, so that it was spotlessly clean and the fur gleaming. She happened to be sitting in the bottom of her cage, having a sun bath, her lovely tail dangling through the wire, when the bandits appeared on the scene.

One of them found this long, silky tail lying on the ground and, as it did not appear to belong to anyone, and it seemed as though it might be good to eat, he rushed at it and sank his teeth into it. The other two, seeing what he had found, immediately joined him and laid hold as well. The monkey was terribly frightened and scrambled up to the top of her cage, screaming loudly, but this did not shake off the bandits; they clung on like a vice and the higher the monkey climbed up the cage, the higher her tail lifted them off the ground, so that when I arrived on the scene, they were about a foot in the air, revolving slowly round and round, all growling together with their jaws still firmly locked to the monkey's tail. It took me several minutes to get them to let go, and then they only did so because I blew clouds of cigarette smoke in their faces, and made them cough.

Not long after this, the bandits did very much the same sort of thing to me. Every morning when I had given them their breakfast, I would let them wander around my bed until my tea arrived. They

would investigate the bed very thoroughly, grunting and squeaking to each other, trotting up and down and sticking their long, pink noses into every fold of the sheets to make sure nothing eatable was hidden there.

On this particular morning I was lying there half asleep while the bandits scrambled all over the bed and did mountaineering tricks on the blanket. Suddenly I felt an agonizing pain in my foot. I shot up in bed and discovered that one of the bandits had been nosing round and uncovered my toe. This, he thought, was some delicacy I had concealed for his special benefit.

Greedy, as usual, he had tried to get as much of my toe as possible into his mouth, and was busily chewing at it, uttering delighted grunts when I caught him by the tail and hauled him off. He was most reluctant to let go: in fact, he seemed extremely annoyed at being disturbed in the middle of what was obviously going to be a wonderful meal.

Eventually, the bandits grew too big to be kept in a basket and I had to move them to a cage. Actually, the real reason was that they had bitten such huge holes in the wickerwork that there was hardly any basket left to keep them in. They had by this time learnt to feed out of a dish and were eating raw eggs and finely chopped meat mixed up with their milk. I built them a very nice cage and they thoroughly approved of it. It had a bedroom at one end for them to sleep in, and the rest of the cage was used for feeding and playing in. There were two doors, one at each end of the cage, leading into the bedroom and playground. I had hoped that once they were settled in this new home, I would have no more trouble with them, but I was very much mistaken. The problem now was to feed them.

Their cage was on top of a whole pile of others containing various creatures, and so it was quite high off the ground. As soon as they saw me approaching with the food dish, they would all start screaming as loudly as they could, and would cluster round the door, poking their long, pink noses through the wire. They would be so excited at the idea of a meal, and each one so determined to get to the food plate first, that as soon as I opened the door of the cage, they would hurl themselves through it, screaming and yelling, knock the plate of food out of my hand and fall to the ground below with a crash. I let them do this twice, thinking that after the second fall they would have learnt not to rush out the moment the door was opened, but it was no use. They would shoot out like rockets, the plate would go flying and they would land on the floor snorting and biting wildly.

Then I would have to pick them up, put them back in their cage and go and prepare another plateful of food. When they were as excited as this, you had to be very careful how you picked them up as well, for they used to bite at anything and everything within reach.

At last I grew tired of having the bandits falling out of their cage at every mealtime, so I invented a rather cunning plan.

I would go to the cage with their food dish as usual, they would cluster round the door, waiting their chance to dash out. Then I would get somebody to go to the other end of the cage and rattle the door leading to their bedroom. As soon as they heard this, they would think the food dish was being put in there and would scramble off down the cage, screaming and growling, and disappear into the bedroom. When they were safely out of sight, I had to open the other door; they would realize they had been fooled and come dashing out of their bedroom again. Then, if I had not got my hand outside, they would probably fasten on to my fingers and hang on for all they were worth.

These little animals probably caused me more trouble and gave me more bites and scratches than any other creatures I have collected. But even so, I could not help getting fond of them. I knew they did not bite me because they were nasty-tempered, but simply because they became over-excited and mistook me for bits of a meal. I used to get extremely angry with them sometimes and think how nice it would be if I handed them over to a zoo, for somebody else to be worried and bitten by them. But when at last that time came and I handed them over to the zoo where they were going to live, I really felt sorry to see them go.

I went and took a last look at them in their big zoo cage, and they appeared so innocent and sweet, trotting round on the sawdust, wiffling their stupid-looking noses, that I wondered if perhaps I had misjudged them. I began to feel very sad at the thought of parting with them. I called them over to the wire to say good-bye and they looked so quiet and good that I poked my finger through the bars to scratch their heads for the last time. I should really have known better. They changed at once from innocent-looking little animals to the screeching bandits I knew of old, and before I could remove my finger, they had all fastened on to it, in a bunch.

When I eventually got free, I walked away from the cage, mopping up the blood with my handkerchief and deciding that I was, after all, very glad that somebody else was going to look after them in the future.

CHAPTER FIVE

In which I become involved with a number of monkeys

A GREAT many people, both European and African, used to come to the camp site, to have a look round and see all the strange animals that I had collected. Among these varied creatures, there were, of course, the monkeys, of which we had about fifty different kinds. Sharing even such a big thing as a marquee with many of these lively animals was an exhausting experience, for fifty monkeys can create an awful lot of trouble when they give their minds to it.

Of all the monkeys we had, there are three that I remember best. These were Footle, the moustached monkey, Weekes, the red-headed mangabey, and, last but not last, Cholmondely, the chimpanzee.

Footle, when he arrived in the camp, was the smallest monkey I had ever seen, for, with the exception of his long tail, he would fit very comfortably into a teacup, and then leave a certain amount of room to spare. His fur was a peculiar shade of green, and he had a very nice white shirt front; his head, like those of most baby monkeys, seemed much too big for his body and it was the same greenish colour, except for his cheeks, which were a bright buttercup yellow. But the most astonishing thing about him was the broad curved band of white fur across his upper lip, which made him look exactly as though he possessed a big moustache. I had never seen anything quite so ridiculous as this tiny monkey wearing this enormous Santa-Claus-like decoration on his face.

For the first few days, Footle lived in a basket by my bed with other baby animals, and had to be fed with milk from a feeding bottle. The bottle was about twice his size, and he used to fling himself on it with cries of joy when it arrived, stuff the end into his mouth, and wrap his arms and legs round it firmly, so that I could not take it away before he had finished. He would not even let me hold the bottle for him, presumably in case I stole any of the contents, and so he would roll about on the bed with it clutched in his arms, looking just as if he were wrestling with an airship. Sometimes he would be on top, sometimes the bottle, but whether he was on top or underneath, Footle would still suck away at the milk, his moustache jerking up and down with the effort.

He was a very intelligent little monkey and it was not very long before he had learned to drink his milk out of a saucer but as soon as this had been mastered, his table manners became simply frightful. I would put him on the table to be fed, and when he saw me approaching with the saucer he would work himself up into a frenzy of impatience, jumping up and down with excitement and screaming at the top of his voice. Hardly was his meal on the table, than he would without any hesitation dive head first into it. There would be a great shower of milk and he would sit in the centre of it and duck his head under the surface, only coming up when he could not hold his breath any longer. Occasionally, in his greed, he would wait too long and come up sputtering and sneezing out milk like a fountain. It used to take me a good half an hour to dry him after every meal, for by the time he had finished, he would look as though he had been bathing in the milk instead of drinking it.

I decided that this could not go on, for Footle was fed five times a day and, as he got soaked each time, I was frightened that he might catch a chill.

I thought that the reason for his excitement was that he could see the milk coming when he was sitting on the table, so I tried a new way of feeding him. I put the saucer on the table first and then carried Footle to it. The first time I did this, he saw the milk when he was still some way off and, uttering a shrill squeal of joy, he jumped out of my hands, shot through the air very gracefully, and landed in the centre of the milk with a splash. Of course, the saucer was overturned and both Footle and I were drenched.

After this, I tried holding him while he drank, and this was a trifle more successful. He used to wriggle and scream with rage because I would not let him dive into the milk as though it were a swimming pool, and sometimes he would succeed and struggle free, plunging in before I could stop him. But on most occasions, this method worked well and he remained reasonably dry, except of course for his face. I was unable to stop him pushing that into the milk, and when he came up for air his face would be so white with cream that you could not tell where his moustache began and ended.

When Footle was not eating, he loved to cling to something. All baby monkeys, when they are that age, usually cling to the soft fur of their mother as she wanders through the trees. Footle, having adopted me as his mother, seemed to think that it was only right that he should cling to me when he was not feeding. Most of the time I used to carry him around when I worked, and he behaved very well, sitting on my shoulder, and clinging to my ear with one hand. But one day he got too brave and jumped off, to land on the wire front of a cage which contained a large and fierce monkey, which promptly grabbed Footle by the tail. If I had not been there to rescue him, this would have been his last adventure.

I decided that it was too dangerous for Footle to sit on my shoulder while I worked, and therefore I shut him up in his basket, but he was obviously unhappy and spent his day screaming plaintively and trying to climb out, so I had to think of something else. I got an old coat of mine and wore it for a few days, carrying him around on my shoulder as usual. When he had become quite used to the garment, I took it off and hung it over the back of a chair and then put Footle on to it. He did not seem to realize that

I was no longer inside the coat and clung to it with great affection.

So every morning I would put the coat over the back of the chair, place Footle on it and he would cling there quite happily while I got on with my work. He seemed to think that the coat was part of me, a sort of extra skin I suppose, and as long as he was attached to some part of me he felt quite happy. He would even carry on long squeaking conversations with me while I worked, but never attempted to leave the coat and climb up on to my shoulder.

When he eventually arrived back at Liverpool, Footle had a wonderful time posing on my shoulder for the press-photographers. They were quite fascinated by him; none of them had ever seen such a tiny monkey. One reporter watched him for a long time, and then he turned to me and said, 'You know, he seems awfully young to have such a big moustache.'

Weekes, the red-headed mangabey, came by his name owing to his cry. Whenever you went near his cage, he would open his mouth wide and shout 'Weekes, weekes' at the top of his voice.

He was a delicate shade of grey all over, except for a band of white fur round his neck, and the top of his head, which was a bright mahogany red. His face was a very dark grey and his eyelids were creamy white. Normally, you could not see these, but when he greeted you he would raise his eyebrows and lower his lids so suddenly, it looked as though his eyes had been covered by white shutters.

Weekes was very bored with living in a cage by himself with no one to play with, but I could not give him a mate, as he was the only one of his species that I had. He did not realize this, however, for all round him he could hear and smell other monkeys and he thought it very unfair of me not to let him leave his cage and go to play with them. He decided the best thing to do was to tunnel his way out of the side when I was not looking.

He had discovered a small gap between the boards of the side of his cage and set to work with fingers and teeth to widen it. The wood was very hard, and it was only after much picking and biting that he was able to work off a small splinter. I kept a cautious eye on the hole to make sure it did not get any larger, but Weekes did not know this and thought I knew nothing about it. He would spend hours biting and scratching at the wood, but as soon as he heard me coming he would leap up on to his perch and sit there, looking as innocent as possible, raising his eyebrows and showing his white eyelids, blinking at me cheerfully, in the hope of persuading me that he was the very last monkey in the camp to do anything wicked.

I did not do anything about Weekes's hole, for I thought that as soon as he found out how hard the wood was he would soon give it up. To my surprise, exactly the opposite happened. He became so interested that he used to spend every available moment biting and scratching and sucking at the wood. Every time I came on the scene, however, there he was sitting on his perch without a care in the world, and if it had not been for the few splinters that stuck to the hairs of his chin, I should not have known that he was still going on with his mining operations. He seemed so convinced that I did not know about his secret passage that one day I thought I would give him a surprise.

I had just given him a bowl of milk, so he was not expecting me back at his cage for at least an hour. Refreshed by his drink, he set to work on his hole. I allowed him enough time to get well started and then I crept down the line of cages. There was Weekes, squatting on the floor, with a grim, determined expression on his face, tugging with both

hands at quite a large splinter of wood. It was a very tough piece, and although he pulled at it with all his might, it would not part company with the side of the cage, and so he became angrier and angrier, muttering to himself and screwing up his face in the most frightening grimaces. Just as he was bending forwards to see if he could bite through the annoying splinter, I asked him in a stern voice what he thought he was doing.

He jumped as though I had jabbed him with a pin, and then glanced over his shoulder with a horrified and guilty expression on his face. I asked him again what he thought he was up to, and, giving me a feeble grin, he made a half-hearted attempt to show me his eyelids. Seeing that I was not to be distracted, he sheepishly let go of the splinter and seizing his empty milk pot, leapt on to his perch, where he was overcome with embarrassment and put the pot over his face and fell backwards off the perch on to the bottom of the cage.

He looked so ridiculous that I had to laugh, and so he decided that I must have forgiven him. He climbed back on to his perch, wearing the pot like a tin helmet on his head, and then fell off the perch again. This time he fell on his head and hurt himself, so he had to come to the bars and have his paws held until he felt better.

Now he realized I knew all about his hole, he gave up being so secretive about it and used to work away in full view of me. If I scolded him, he would repeat his trick of putting the pot over his face and falling backwards off the perch; and if I laughed he would assume that he had been forgiven and go back to work. Just as a precaution, however, I nailed a bit of wire over the outside of his hole, which he was extremely annoyed about when he discovered it. When he found he could not shift the wire, he rather reluctantly gave up his tunnelling, but never forgot his trick of falling off his perch backwards, and would always do it when he knew I was angry with him, in order to try to pacify me.

CHAPTER SIX

The story of Cholmondely the chimpanzee

WHEN Cholmondely, the chimpanzee, joined the collection, he immediately became the uncrowned king of it, not only because of his size, but also because he was so remarkably intelligent. Cholmondely had been the pet of a district officer who, wanting to send the ape to the London Zoo, and hearing that I was collecting wild animals in that region and would shortly be returning to England, wrote and asked me if I would mind taking Cholmondely with me and handing him over to the Zoo authorities. I wrote back to say that, as I already had a large collection of monkeys, another chimpanzee would not make any difference, so I would gladly escort Cholmondely back to England. I imagined that he would be quite a young chimp, perhaps two years old, and standing about two feet high. When he arrived I got a considerable shock.

A small van drew up outside the camp one morning and in the back of it was an enormous wooden crate. It was big enough, I thought, to house an elephant. I wondered what on earth could be inside, and when the driver told me that it contained Cholmondely I remember thinking how silly his owner was to send such a small chimpanzee in such a huge crate. I opened the door and looked inside and there sat Cholmondely.

One glance at him and I realized that this was no

baby chimpanzee but a fully-grown one about eight or nine years old. Sitting hunched up in the dark crate, he looked as though he were about twice as big as I, and from the expression on his face I gathered that the trip had not been to his liking. Before I could shut the door of the box, however, Cholmondely had extended a long, hairy arm, clasped my hand in his and shaken it warmly. Then he turned round and gathered up a great length of chain (one end of which was fastened to a collar round his neck), draped it carefully over his arm, and stepped down, out of the box. He stood there for a moment and, after surveying me carefully, examined the camp with great interest, whereupon he held out his hand, looking at me inquiringly. I took it in mine and we walked into the marquee together.

Cholmondely immediately went and seated himself on one of the chairs by the camp table, dropped his chain on the floor and sat back and crossed his legs. He gazed round the tent for a few minutes with a rather supercilious expression on his face, and evidently deciding that it would do he turned and looked at me inquiringly again. Obviously, he wanted me to offer him something after his tiring journey. I had been warned before he arrived that he was a hardened tea drinker, and so I called out to the cook and told him to make a pot of tea. Then I went out and had a look in Cholmondely's crate, and in the bottom I found an enormous and very battered tin mug. When I returned to the tent with this, Cholmondely was quite overjoyed and even praised me for my cleverness in finding it, by uttering a few cheerful 'hoo hoo' noises.

While we were waiting for the tea to arrive, I sat

down opposite Cholmondely and lit a cigarette. To my surprise, he became very excited and held out his hand across the table to me. Wondering what he would do, I handed him the cigarette packet. He opened it, took out a cigarette, and put it between his lips. He then reached out his hand again and I gave him the matches; to my astonishment, he took one out of the box, struck it, lit his cigarette, and threw the box down on the table. Lying back in his chair he blew out clouds of smoke in the most professional manner.

No one had told me that Cholmondely smoked. I wondered rather anxiously what other bad habits he might have which his master had not warned me about.

Just at that moment, the tea was brought in and Cholmondely greeted its appearance with loud and expressive hoots of joy. He watched me carefully while I half-filled his mug with milk and then added the tea. I had been told that he had a very sweet tooth, so I put in six large spoons of sugar, an action which he greeted with grunts of satisfaction. He placed his cigarette on the table and seized the mug with both hands; then he stuck out his lower lip very carefully and dipped it into the tea to make sure it was not too hot.

As it was a trifle warm, he sat there blowing on it vigorously until it was cool enough, and then he drank it all down without stopping once. When he had drained the last drops, he peered into the mug and scooped out all the sugar he could with his forefinger. After that, he tipped the mug up on his nose and sat with it like that for about five minutes until the very last of the sugar had trickled down into his mouth.

I had Cholmondely's big box placed some distance away from the marquee, and fixed the end of his chain to a large tree stump. He was too far away, I thought, to make a nuisance of himself but near enough to be able to watch everything that went on and to conduct long conversations with me in his 'hoo hoo' language.

But on the day of his arrival he caused trouble almost as soon as I had fixed him to his tree stump. Outside the marquee were a lot of small, tame monkeys tied on long strings attached to stakes driven into the ground. They were about ten in number, and over them I had constructed a palm leaf roof as a shelter from the sun. As Cholmondely was examining his surroundings, he noticed these monkeys, some eating fruit and others lying asleep in the sun, and decided he would have a little under-arm bowling practice.

I was working inside the marquee when all at once I heard the most terrific uproar going on outside. The monkeys were screaming and chattering with rage, and I rushed out to see what had happened. Cholmondely, apparently, had picked up a rock the size of a cabbage and hurled it at the smaller monkeys, luckily missing them all, but frightening them out of their wits. If one of them had been hit by such a big rock, it would have been killed instantly.

Just as I arrived on the scene, Cholmondely had picked up another stone and was swinging it backwards and forwards like a professional cricketer, taking better aim. He was annoyed at having missed all the monkeys with his first shot. I grabbed a stick and hurried towards him, shouting, and, to my surprise, Cholmondely dropped the rock and put his arms over his head, and started to roll on the ground and scream. In my haste, I had picked up a very small twig and this made no impression on him at all, for his back was as broad and as hard as a table.

I gave him two sharp cuts with this silly little twig and followed it up with a serious scolding. He sat there picking bits of leaf off his fur and looking very guilty. With the aid of the Africans, I set to work and cleared away all the rocks and stones near his box, and, giving him another scolding, went back to my work. I hoped that this telling-off might have some effect on him, but when I looked out of the marquee some time later, I saw him digging in the earth, presumably in search of more ammunition.

Not long after his arrival at the camp, Cholmondely, to my alarm, fell ill. For nearly two weeks he went off his food, refusing even the most tempting fruit and other delicacies, and even rejecting his daily ration of tea, a most unheard-of occurrence. All he had was a few sips of water every day, and gradually he grew thinner and thinner, his eyes sank into their sockets, and I really thought he was going to die. He lost all interest in life and sat hunched up in his box all day, with his eyes closed. It was very bad for him to spend all day moping in this fashion, so in the evenings, just before the sun went down, when it was cool, I used to make him come out for walks with me. These walks were only short, and we had to rest every few yards, for Cholmondely was weak with lack of food.

One evening, just before I took him out for a walk, I filled my pockets with a special kind of biscuit that he had been very fond of. We went slowly up to the top of a small hill just beyond the camp and then sat there to admire the view. As we rested, I took a biscuit out of my pocket and ate it, smacking my lips with enjoyment, but not offering any to Cholmondely. He looked very surprised, for he knew that I always shared my food with him when we were out together. I ate a second biscuit and he watched me closely to see if I enjoyed it as much as the first. When he saw that I did, he dipped his hand into my pocket, pulled out a biscuit, smelled it suspiciously, and then, to my delight, ate it up and started looking for another. I knew then that he was going to get better.

The next morning he drank a mugful of sweet tea and ate seventeen biscuits, and for three days lived entirely on this diet. After this his appetite returned with a rush, and for the next fortnight he ate twice as much as he had ever done before, and cost me a small fortune in bananas.

There were only two things that Cholmondely disliked. One of them was the Africans and the other, snakes. I think that when he was a baby some Africans must have teased him. Whatever the reason, however, he certainly got his own back on more than one occasion. He would hide inside the box and wait until an African passed close by and then he would rush out with all his hair standing on end, swinging his long arms and screaming in the most terrifying manner. Many a fat African woman carrying a basket of fruit on her head would chance to pass too closely to Cholmondeley's box, and would have to drop her basket, pick up her skirts, and run for dear life, while Cholmondely danced victoriously at the end of his chain, hooting and showing all his teeth in a grin of delight.

With snakes, of course, he was not nearly so brave. If he saw me handling one, he would get very agitated, wringing his hands and moaning with fear, and if I put the reptile on the ground and it started to crawl towards him, he would run to the very end of his chain and scream loudly for help, throwing bits of stick and grass at the snake to try and stop it coming any closer.

One night, I went to shut him up in his box, as usual, and, to my surprise, he flatly refused to go into it. His bed of banana leaves was nicely made, and so I thought he was simply being naughty, but when I started to scold him, he took me by the hand, led me up to his box and left me there while he retreated to the safety of the end of his chain, and stood watching me anxiously. I realized there must be something inside, of which he was frightened, and when I cautiously investigated I found a very small snake coiled up in the centre of his bed. After I had captured it, I found that it was a harmless type; Cholmondely, of course, could not tell the difference, and he was taking no chances.

Cholmondely was so quick at learning tricks and so willing to show off that when he returned to England he became quite famous and even made several appearances on television, delighting the audiences by sitting on a chair, with a hat on, taking a cigarette and lighting it for himself, pouring out and drinking a glass of beer, and many other things.

I think he must have become rather swollen-headed with his success, for not long after this he managed to escape from the zoo and went wandering off by himself through Regent's Park, much to the horror of everyone he met. On reaching the main road, he found a bus standing there and promptly climbed aboard, for he loved being taken for a ride. The passengers, however, decided they would rather not travel by that particular bus if Cholmondely was going to use it as well, and they were all struggling to get out when some keepers arrived from the zoo and took Cholmondely in charge.

He was marched back to his cage in disgrace, but if I know Cholmondely, he must have thought it worth any amount of scoldings just for the sight of all those people trying to get off the bus together, and getting stuck in the door. Cholmondely had a great sense of humour.

CHAPTER SEVEN

Problems of hairy frogs, tortoises, and other beasts

CATCHING your animals is generally, but not always, the easiest part of a collecting trip. Once you have caught them, your job is to keep them alive and well in captivity, and this is not always so easy. Animals react in various ways to captivity, and you will even get individuals of the same species that seem to have totally different outlooks. Sometimes they will differ in quite small things and at other times their reactions will be so dissimilar that you would think they might be two separate species.

I once bought two baby drills from a hunter. Drills are those large, grey-coloured baboons with pink behinds that you can see in most zoological gardens. These two babies settled down very well but they differed in a lot of small habits. For example, when they were given bananas, one of them would carefully peel the fruit and eat it, throwing away the skin, while the other would peel his banana just as carefully, eat the skin, and throw away the fruit.

With the monkey collection one of the most important items of their diet was the milk that they got every night. This was dried milk that I would mix up in a big kerosene tin full of hot water; then I would stir in several calcium tablets and a number of spoonfuls of malt and cod-liver oil mixture, so the resulting drink looked not unlike weak coffee. Most of the babies I had took this drink immediately and would go absolutely mad when they saw the pots arriving at feeding time. They would shake the bars and scream and shout, and stamp on the floor of their cages with excitement as they saw me pouring out the milk. The adult monkeys, however, took quite a long time to become used to this curious pale brown liquid. They seemed to be extremely suspicious of it, for some reason.

Sometimes I managed to get a newly-arrived monkey to drink this mixture by turning its cage round so that it could see all the other monkeys busily guzzling and hiccupping over their milk pots. The new arrival would then become curious and decide that perhaps the stuff in his pot was worth investigating. Once he had tasted it, he would very soon grow just as enthusiastic over it as the rest of the monkeys.

Occasionally, however, I would get an extremely stubborn animal that would refuse even to taste his milk, in spite of watching all the others drinking theirs. I found the only thing to do in this case was to take a cupful of milk and throw it over the monkey's hands and feet. As they are extremely clean creatures, he would get to work to remove the sticky liquid from his fur by licking it, and once he had got the taste and smell of the milk he would then drink it readily out of a pot.

With most animals, feeding is fairly straightforward if you know what they eat in the wild state. The meat-eating animals, for example, such as the mongooses or the wild cats, can be fed on goat or cow meat, raw egg and a certain amount of milk. The important thing with these animals is to make sure that they have plenty of roughage. When they kill their prey in the wild state, they will eat the skin, bones, and all; so if they are used to having this roughage, they soon sicken and die should it be withheld from them in captivity. I used to keep a big basketful of feathers and fur, and I would drop pieces of goat or cow meat into it and get them all covered with feathers and bits of fur before giving them to the mongooses.

I came across this same problem of supplying roughage to birds of prey. Owls, for example, will eat a mouse, and then some time later sick up the bones and the skin, in the form of an oval pellet. When you keep owls in captivity, you always have to make sure they are regularly producing these pellets, which are called castings, as this is a sure sign the bird is in good health.

Once, when I was hand-rearing some baby owls, I could get no roughage that I thought was suitable for them, and so I was forced to wrap small pieces of meat in cotton-wool and push them down their ever-open beaks. This worked very well, somewhat to my surprise, and the little owls produced pellets composed entirely of cotton-wool, for a number of weeks. Their cage looked rather as though they had been having a snowball fight, with all these little white castings lying about on the floor.

The animals which cause the collector most trouble are those species which have a restricted diet in the wild state. For example, in West Africa live the pangolins or scaly ant-eaters, great creatures that have long pointed noses and long tails, with which they can hang from the branches of trees. They are covered with large, strong-overlapping scales so that they look like strangely-shaped fir cones. In the wilds these animals feed solely on the ants' nests which are built among the branches.

While I was keeping these animals in Africa, I could quite easily have given them an endless supply of their natural food, but, unfortunately, you cannot do this when the animal is in England. So you have to teach the animal to eat a substitute food, something that will be easily obtainable in the zoo to which it is going. It is no use landing in England an ant-eater that will only eat ants, as there is no zoo that would be able to supply them.

My scaly ant-eater had to be taught to eat a mixture of unsweetened condensed milk, finely shredded raw meat, and raw egg, mixed up together in a sloppy paste. They are extremely stupid animals and it gener-

ally took them several weeks to learn to feed on this mixture properly. For the first few days of their capture, they would generally overturn their pot of food, unless you tied it in place.

One of the most difficult creatures I had to deal with was a very rare animal known as the giant water shrew. This is a long black beast with a mass of white whiskers and a curious leathery tail like a tadpole's, that lives in the fast-running streams of the West African forest. Like ant-eaters, it had an extremely restricted diet in the wild state, feeding only upon the big brown fresh-water crabs which are so plentiful in its natural habitat. When I obtained my first giant water shrew, I fed him on crabs for two or three days until he had settled down and got used to his cage. Then I set about the task of trying to teach him to eat a substitute food on which he could live in England.

From a local market, I obtained a large number of dried shrimps which the natives use in their food. These I crumbled up and mixed with a little raw egg and finely-chopped meat. Then I got the body of a large crab, cut it in half, scooped out the inside and stuffed it full of the mixture. I joined the two halves together again and, waiting until the giant water shrew was really hungry, threw this false crab into his cage. He jumped for it, gave two swift bites, which was his normal method of dispatching a crab, and stopped and sniffed suspiciously: obviously, this crab did not taste like the ones to which he was used. He sniffed again and thought about it for a bit, and must then have decided the taste was quite pleasant, so he set to work and had soon eaten it up. For several weeks after this he had a number of real crabs and a number of specially stuffed ones every day until he got quite used to the taste of the new food. Then I started to put my substitute food mixture in a pot, with the body of a crab on top. While he was biting the crab, he discovered the food underneath, and, after repeating this experiment for a couple of days, he was taking the mixture out of the pot without any trouble at all.

When an animal was brought in, I could usually tell, more or less, what type of food it was going to require, but I always asked the native hunter, who made the capture, if he knew what the animal ate, in case it had been noticed eating some particular food in the forest, which would help me to vary its diet in captivity. As a rule, however, the hunters had not even the faintest idea what half their captives ate, and, if they did not know, they would just simply say the beast ate banga, the nut of the palm-oil tree. Sometimes this would be quite correct, as in the case of the rats, mice, and squirrels. But on more than one occasion I had been assured by the native hunter that such unlikely things as snakes or small birds lived on this diet. I became so used to this that whenever a hunter told me the animal he had brought in lived entirely on palm nuts, I disbelieved him automatically.

One day I obtained four lovely forest tortoises which were in the best of health and which settled down very well in a little fenced yard that I built for them. Now, as a rule, tortoises are one of the simplest creatures to feed. They will eat almost any form of leaf or vegetable that you give them, together with fruit, and, in some cases, a small piece of raw meat occasionally. However, these tortoises proved to be the exception to the rule. They refused all the delicacies that I showered on them, turned up their noses at all the ripe fruit and tender leaves which I took such pains to get for them. I could not understand it and began to worry quite a bit about them.

One day a native hunter came to the camp and, while I was showing him the collection and telling him which animals were wanted, I called his attention to these tortoises and to the fact that ever since I had got them, some two or three weeks previously, they had refused to eat anything. Whereupon he promptly turned round and told me I was giving the tortoises all the wrong things to eat and that they did not eat fruit or leaves. He insisted they lived on a species of tiny white forest mushrooms which grew on dead tree trunks in the forest. To be perfectly honest I did not believe him, although I did not say so. I thought this was just another way of saying that the creatures lived on palm nuts.

However, another week passed and still my tortoises had eaten nothing, so in desperation I sent two small boys out into the forest with a basket and instructed them to bring me as many of these small white mush-

rooms as they could find. When they returned I emptied the basketful of mushrooms into the tortoises' pen and stood by, to watch. I do not think that I have ever seen tortoises move so fast towards food. They scuttled across the compound and within a very few minutes were chewing happily away at the mushrooms with the juice running down their chins. Strangely enough, once they had been fed on mushrooms, they started eating the other food as well, and before many weeks had passed they had completely given up eating mushrooms altogether and much preferred a nice ripe mango.

As my collection grew, it became quite a problem to maintain a good supply of food for so many animals with such varied likes and dislikes. Meat, fruit, eggs, and chickens I obtained from the local market but there were other things that I had to have.

For example, all the birds, most of the monkeys, and such things as the galagos and some of the forest rats, adored grasshoppers and locusts, and in order to keep them in good health it was necessary to have a constant supply of these delicacies for them. As you cannot buy grasshoppers and locusts in even a West African market, my own special team of grasshopper capturers had to be organized. This consisted of ten small boys who had quick eyes and could run very fast.

I supplied each of them with a large cigarette tin and a butterfly net, and twice a day they would go off and capture as many grasshoppers and locusts as they could with the nets, push them into the cigarette tin and bring them back to camp. They were paid not by the amount of time they spent on the job, but by the number of grasshoppers they procured. The average payment was five grasshoppers to the penny, and some of these little boys, who were quicker than the others and more agile, could earn as much as three or four shillings a day.

The native name for grasshoppers is 'pampalo', and

this team of little boys became known to me as the 'pampalo catchers', so if an animal was looking sick, or a newly-caught one arrived and was in need of some delicacy to soothe his ruffled feelings after capture, I would shout out for the pampalo catchers and they would all set off into the grass fields to bring in a fresh supply of insects.

To supply all the birds I had with insects was even more of a problem, as the majority of them were too small to be able to cope with the big prickly grass-hoppers. The thing they liked best was a sort of white baby termite, or white ant, and I had to employ another team of boys to get these for me. There are several different sorts of white ant found in West Africa, but the one that I found most useful was known as the 'Mushroom' termite. In cool glades among the big forest trees they built the most peculiar nests out of grey mud. These nests looked exactly like giant toadstools, standing about two feet high. The interior of such a nest is like a honeycomb, filled with tiny passages and little cells in which the worker termites and the baby termites live. My team of termite hunters would go off into the forest in the early morning and return in the evening with three or four nests each, perched on their woolly heads.

These nests I stored in a cool, dark place, and when it was feeding time for the birds I would spread a big canvas sheet on the ground and carefully split open the nests with a chopper. Then I would shake them and from the inside would pour a stream of termites both large and small, which I would shovel into pots and push hastily into the bird cages before the termites crawled out. All the birds realized the necessity for speed, and no sooner had the door closed behind my hands than they would be perched on the edge of the tin pecking away for dear life.

Quite apart from this problem of feeding so many different kinds of animals when collected, there was the job of caging them correctly. Each kind of animal had to have its own special sort of cage, and it had to be designed and built with very great care. It had to be made so that it was cool while in the tropics and yet kept the animals warm when the ship drew nearer to England. As an added precaution, I used to make a curtain of sacking for each cage which I could lower over the bars in front, so that if there was a cold wind blowing, or it was raining, the animal inside would be protected.

Then there was the problem of size. Sometimes quite a small creature needs a very large cage, to keep it healthy. Sometimes quite a large animal has to be kept in quite a small cage for the same reason. For instance, the galagos had to have ample space to allow them to leap about and run round and round, as in the wild state they are constantly on the move, and keeping them in small cages would prevent them from getting the right amount of exercise.

On the other hand, some beautiful, spotted antelopes which I collected, called water chevrotains, had to be kept in long narrow boxes which did not allow them to turn round. The sides of these boxes had to be padded with sacking stuffed with cotton-wool. The reason for this was the extreme nervousness of these animals, and when the cage was rattling and bumping long in the lorry, or being hoisted on or off a steamer, the antelopes were liable to get very frightened. If the cage had been square they would have run round and round inside it and eventually lost their balance and fallen and probably broken their very slender, fragile legs. In the long narrow cage, however, they could brace themselves against the padded sides when there was any movement, and so there was no chance of their falling down and breaking a limb. The padded sides, of course, were to prevent them from being rubbed sore against the woodwork.

Strangely enough, another creature that had to have a padded box was a fantastic kind of frog I caught, called the hairy frog. These chocolate-coloured amphibians have the rear end of their bodies and their fat thighs covered with a thick growth of what looks exactly like hair. In reality, it is long, slender filaments of skin. All frogs to a certain extent breathe through their skins, as well as with the aid of their lungs. That is why it is necessary to keep a frog in a moist condition, otherwise his skin will dry up and he will suffocate.

Hairy frogs live in very fast-running mountain streams and spend most of their time submerged below the water. Therefore, they do not use their lungs for breathing quite as much as the normal frog will do, and in consequence they need a considerably greater area of skin to enable them to breathe under water. So they have evolved the 'hairs'.

These strange frogs created quite a problem in housing. Most frogs you keep in a shallow box until such time as you are going to get on the ship, when you place each one of them inside a butter-muslin bag and hang it on the side of a big box. They sit in these bags quite happily till you reach England. They do not want much food on the voyage: as long as they are wet two or three times a day they are perfectly satisfied.

The hairy frogs possess, as well as the strange decoration on their rears, another peculiar feature. In the fleshy toes of their hind feet they have long, sharp claws very like the claws of a cat, which, moreover, they can pull back into the sheath as a cat can. Now, if you put hairy frogs inside the usual butter-muslin bag they try to hop; their claws come out of the sheath and get stuck in the muslin, and within a very short time your frogs are twisted in the most dreadful knot in the bottom of the bag. I decided, therefore, that the frogs would have to travel in a box.

Now another problem made itself apparent. The box had to be extremely shallow, otherwise the frogs, when frightened, would jump wildly into the air and hit their heads on the wire top. Consequently, I put all the hairy frogs in a shallow wooden box with holes bored in the bottom, so that when I watered them the liquid would run out. Since they could not jump, the hairy frogs developed a new habit: whenever they were frightened, they would rush into a corner and try to burrow into the woodwork. After a couple of days of this they had worn all the skin off their noses and upper lips.

This is an extremely dangerous thing to happen to a frog, for these rubbed spots can quickly develop into a great sore which will, if it is not treated, eventually eat away the nose and upper lip. Treatment for any sort of wound on a frog is made doubly difficult by the fact that you are forced to keep the beast moist, and, of course, a cut or a sore that is moist will take three times as long to heal. So I not only had to design a new cage for the hairy frogs, but I also had to think of some way of healing their noses, without causing them any discomfort.

I built them a large shallow box, and the whole of the inside was covered with thin sheet material stuffed with cotton-wool, so that the walls, floor, and ceiling of the box were quilted – as though they were covered with an eiderdown. I put the hairy frogs in this, and instead of watering them three times a day, as usual, I only watered them once a day. I found this was very successful, for the cotton-wool inside the padding soaked up the water which kept the interior of the box reasonably moist, without actually letting the frogs become too wet. Eventually, the sores on their noses healed up perfectly and they travelled safely to England inside their padded boxes where they could do no damage to themselves, for when they jumped or burrowed they met only the soft surface of the cotton-wool padding.

CHAPTER EIGHT

In which the new Noah sets sail in his ark

THE time that the collector dreads most on a trip is when it is necessary to pack up his great array of animals and transport them down to the coast and on to the ship for the long voyage back to England. First of all, you have to make sure that every cage is in good repair and every door secure. Then, make arrangements for the food supply needed on the ship, for you cannot board even the most well-conducted boat and expect the cook to cater for a hundred-odd animals.

Quite apart from such things as sacks of wheat, potatoes, cocoa yams, and other curious tropical vegetables, you have to have an enormous supply of fruit. It is quite useless to buy all this fruit when it is ripe, for after the first week of the voyage you would find that it had by then gone rotten and none would be left on which to feed your animals. So you have to divide your fruit into three sections – ripe, half ripe, and completely unripe. The unripe fruit, together with the meat and eggs, has to be stored in the ship's refrigerator.

This will keep meat and eggs from going bad and also prevent the fruit from becoming ripe; so when you have used up your ripe fruit you fetch a fresh supply out of the refrigerator and lay it on deck, in the sun, where it ripens very quickly and can be fed to the animals. You have to work out your quantities of food very carefully. If too much is taken, you will find that a lot of it will go bad and will have to be thrown overboard.

On the other hand, should you take too little, you will run out just as you reach a place like the Bay of Biscay where good food and plenty of it is essential if you want the animals to survive the sudden change in climate. So when you are sure that your caging is complete and food supplies adequate, you can then arrange for the lorries to transport you down country.

When I left West Africa I took with me three sacks of wheat and potatoes, two sacks of cocoa yams, two sacks of corn, fifty pineapples, two hundred oranges, fifty mangoes, and a hundred and fifty great stems of bananas, apart from such things as dried milk, malt, and cod-liver oil, and so on. There were four hundred eggs, each of which had to be carefully tested in a bowl of water to make sure it was fresh before being thoroughly greased and packed in a boxful of straw. For the meat supply, there was a whole bullock and twenty live chickens. This, together with the hundred and fifty-odd cages and all the equipment, was quite a load and I had to hire three lorries and a small van to carry it all down to the coast, two hundred miles away.

I decided to travel by night for several reasons, most important of which was that it was coolest for the animals. If you travel by day, a choice has to be made between two things: putting a tarpaulin over the cages in the back of the lorry and having your animals almost suffocated to death, or else keeping the tarpaulins rolled back and having your animals almost scorched by the cloud of red dust that swirls up behind. So I travelled by night and found it by far the best method.

But you can get very little sleep when being bounced and jolted about in the front of a lorry, and knowing that as soon as dawn comes you have to park by the side of the road and in the shade of the trees unload every single box and crate, and clean and feed all your creatures before you can get any proper sleep yourself. Then, immediately night falls and it grows cool, you load up the lorries and start off once again.

The roads in the Cameroons are so bad that we could not travel at more than twenty-five miles an hour, and so a journey which could have been done in England in one day took us three days to complete.

When I arrived at the coast, I found that the ship had not quite finished loading, which meant that we had to wait before we could take our animals on board, and as it was pouring with rain I decided to leave all the creatures in the lorry until we could do so. Just after I had made this decision, the storm clouds rolled away and the sun shone down on us fiercely, so I had to unload all the animals and carry their cages into the shade of some nearby trees. No sooner had I done this than the storm clouds descended once again and within a few minutes all the cages, the equipment, the food supplies, and myself were drenched with icy rain. After getting aboard, I found every cage filled with sodden shivering animals, and I had to set to work to clean out the lot, replacing the wet sawdust with dry, and throwing handfuls of sawdust over the monkeys, hoping to dry some of the moisture out of their fur, so that they should not catch cold. I then made an extra large supply of hot milk and distributed it to every creature that could take it. Luckily, there were no ill effects from this ducking.

You find that after the first day at sea your animals'

appetites increase tremendously with the sea air, and the monkeys will, if you let them, eat four and five times as much as they normally do. You are supposed to know this before you start on your voyage and to make allowances for it when you are buying the food supplies. Of course, you cannot take with you such delicacies as grasshoppers and termites, but you can get cockroaches for the more delicate birds and animals by going down into the engine-rooms in the evenings and chasing them in and out among the hot pipes. It was not long before the sailors on board ship became quite enthusiastic over this sport and soon we had no reason to go and collect these insects ourselves, for the people from the engine-rooms would bring us a regular supply.

A sea voyage lasting two or three weeks can be very enjoyable, provided that your luggage does not include large quantities of extremely hungry animals. If it does, you will find that you have to work as hard, or harder, than any of the sailors on board ship.

I had to be called at half past five every morning to enable me to get through a lot of the cleaning before breakfast. Then, when I had finished breakfast, I started on the job of feeding the animals, and from then on there was actually not a moment of the day that I could call my own until the last pot of evening milk had been put into the monkeys' cages. As the ship steamed closer and closer to England, the weather became colder and colder, and there were more precautions that had to be taken to ensure that my animals did not catch a chill. Hot milk became the rule every night and the cages had to be carefully covered with tarpaulins and blankets to keep out the cold wind. If there was a rough sea I had to make sure that all the cages were carefully secured to the rails, or else a bad accident might occur.

I had forgotten to do this on the way back from West Africa, and late one night as I was giving the young monkeys the last bottle feed of the day, I noticed the ship was plunging up and down quite vigorously. Looking along my line of cages which were stacked against the rails, I decided that, when I had finished feeding the baby monkeys, I would have to rope them; otherwise, if the weather became worse during the night, they were liable to topple over. No sooner had I made this decision than the ship lurched sickeningly over a particularly big wave and my line of fifty cages toppled and crashed over on their faces on to the deck. I rushed along, lifting them upright and tying them back against the rails, and to my relief, found that none of the inmates was hurt in any way, although the monkeys were extremely indignant and chattered for a long time over the incident.

Sometimes you get other forms of excitement on board ship, when you are travelling with your collection. Coming back from West Africa, I and my friend sailed on a ship whose captain, so people told us, was not at all keen on carrying animals. Naturally, when we heard this, we went out of our way to make as little fuss and trouble as possible, for an irritated captain is a man that no collector likes, as he can make life on board ship very difficult for you and your animals. Well, as usual, when you try to be on your best behaviour for someone, something is sure to go wrong.

The very first morning, my friend threw a large basket of dirty sawdust that we had cleaned out of the cages over the rail into the sea. Unfortunately, he had not made sure which way the wind was blowing and so a huge swirling cloud of dust sailed up into the air and descended on to the bridge where the captain was standing.

This, of course, was not a very good start in our efforts to keep on the right side of him. However, at breakfast, though he greeted us somewhat coldly, he gradually thawed out and, towards the middle of the meal, became quite amiable.

The captain was sitting on one side of the table and I was sitting opposite to him; behind was a series of portholes that looked out on to the hatch where we had all our cages stacked. 'I don't mind what you do,' said the captain to me, 'providing you don't let any of your animals escape.' 'Oh! we shan't do that,' and as I said it, I noticed something moving in the porthole just behind the captain's back. To my horror, I saw that there was a large squirrel. He sat in the porthole and surveyed the dining-saloon with a pleased expression. Then he sat up and started to wash his whiskers.

The captain, meanwhile, continued his breakfast, unaware that there was a squirrel sitting within a yard or so of his neck. When the squirrel had finished washing his whiskers, he looked around him and decided that with so much food on the table the dining-saloon would be a good place for him to investigate, so he peered round for a way down. He had evidently just decided that the best way of reaching the delicacies which he could see, was to jump on to the captain's shoulder and then on to the table, when with a muttered 'Excuse me,' I got up, walked out of the dining-room as nonchalantly as I could, and as soon as I was out of sight of the captain I sprinted hard up on to the deck. I arrived outside the porthole just as the squirrel was bunching himself to spring, and I managed to throw myself across the hatch and grab his big furry tail before he could launch himself on to the captain. I bundled him back into his cage, chattering indignantly, and then I sighed with relief.

When I returned to the dining-room, I found luckily that the captain had not noticed anything and he did not know how close he had been to having a large squirrel land on his neck just as he was in the middle of his bacon and eggs.

As I say, because we wanted to be on our best behaviour nothing seemed to go right. A few days later three large lizards escaped from their box and disappeared rapidly into some large coils of rope lying on the deck. As it was quite impossible to move all that stuff to catch them without the aid of half the ship's company, we had to content ourselves with making grabs at them every time they appeared. At last, after three days, we caught them all, but it was a nerve-racking time, as I was quite convinced that they would somehow or other find their way up on to the bridge and that the captain would see them.

We had only just succeeded in getting the reptiles safely under lock and key, when a monkey escaped. She was a perfectly tame creature and normally would come to you, if you called her, but on this occasion she

was far too interested in exploring the ship to bother about us, and scarcely spared us a few glances even when we tried to lure her back into her cage with a large bunch of golden bananas, a bait which she usually never could resist. That day the ship was pitching and tossing a good deal, and if it had not been for this, I dread to think what would have happened, for the monkey scuttled up the ladder from the well-deck on to the passenger-deck. Luckily there was nobody about and I pursued her, calling in a hoarse whisper. Each time the ship rolled, she was thrown a bit off balance and I would gain a few feet, as I was more used to the movement than the little monkey. She reached the bottom of the staircase leading up to the captain's cabin, and then seeing how close I was, she hesitated for a minute and then turned and ran up the steps towards his half-opened cabin door. I flung myself up the stairs after her, but without much hope, and I could visualize her landing with a thump in the middle of the captain's bed with the captain inside it. Fortunately just as she reached the top step the ship lurched sickenly, and she fell back down three steps which gave me the chance I needed. I grabbed her long furry tail, hoisted her in the air and ran back down into the well-deck as quickly as I could, for I was afraid that her screams of rage would be heard by the captain and bring him out of his cabin to see what was going on.

It was altogether a very trying trip and we were very pleased when, one grey morning, with thin drizzle falling out of the sky, the ship drew into the docks at Liverpool. There on the quay-side were the zoo vans, waiting to collect the specimens. Our collection was unloaded from the ship without any mishap and the animals distributed among the various directors, and we watched them with mixed feelings as they drove off through the rain to their new homes in the various zoos in England.

PART TWO

Hunts and Captures in Guiana

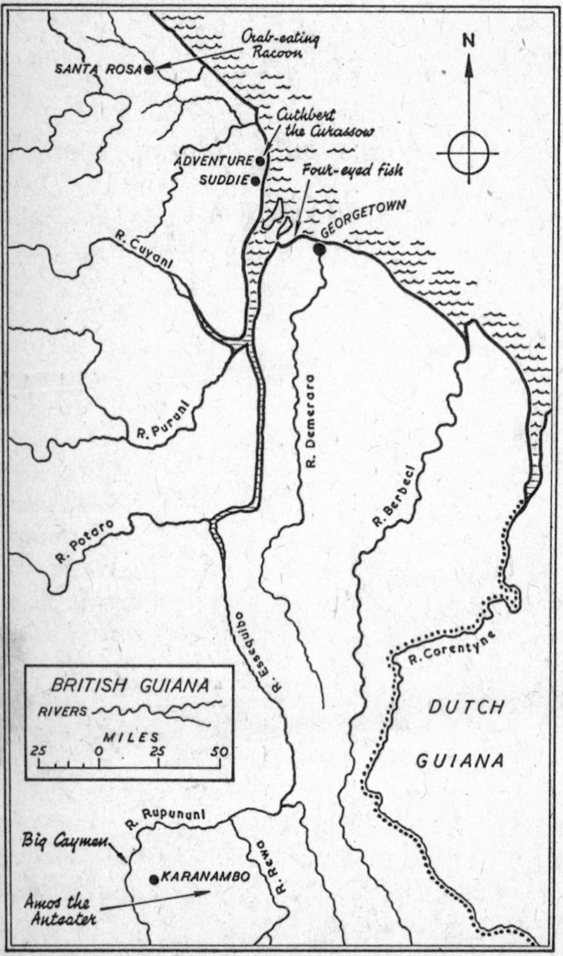

BRITISH GUIANA
RIVERS
MILES
25 0 25 50
N
Crab-eating Racoon
SANTA ROSA
Cuthbert the Curassow
ADVENTURE
SUDDIE
Four-eyed fish
GEORGETOWN
R. Cuyuni
R. Puruni
R. Potaro
R. Demerara
R. Berbeci
R. Essequibo
R. Corentyne
DUTCH GUIANA
R. Rupununi
Big Caymen
KARANAMBO
R. Rewa
Amos the Anteater

CHAPTER NINE

In which Amos the ant-eater leads us a dance

GUIANA is a country lying in the northern half of South America, and is almost as big as Ireland. It is situated on the edge of the great forested region that stretches right along the Amazon and through Brazil. The name Guiana is taken from an Amerindian word meaning the land of water, and it would be difficult to think of a more apt description of the country.

It is split by three great rivers which run down its entire length and which are connected to each other by great numbers of small streams and tributaries. During the rainy season these streams overflow and enormous areas of country are flooded for weeks at a time. Owing to this, we found that nearly all the animals in Guiana were either expert climbers or expert swimmers; animals that in less watery countries spend their whole lives on the ground were here replaced by similar creatures that lived almost entirely in the trees: for example, in the Cameroons you find bush-tailed porcupines which live on the floor of the forest and make their homes among the rocks and caves, and who would find it almost impossible to climb a tree.

In Guiana there are the tree porcupines whose paws are adapted for climbing, and whose long naked tails are prehensile – that is to say, like the South American monkeys, they can wind their tails round the branches to help them in climbing.

We found that Guiana could be roughly divided into two parts. Great forest-lands spread from the shore inland and eventually gave way to extensive savanna-lands where the vegetation was principally grass fields, small clumps of trees, and bushes dotted about it. The Cameroons was, of course, divided in much the same way, and this meant that in both Guiana and the Cameroons you would find one set of animals inhabiting the forest and a totally different set living in the grasslands.

Along the coast of Guiana where the great rivers flow out into the sea, the land is split up by thousands of rivers and creeks. Some are only a few feet wide and some are considerably bigger than the average English river. These creeks provide the most beautiful scenery in Guiana. The waters, filled with dead leaves and logs, are stained a rich sherry-brown colour and their movement is so gentle that the surface is generally as placid as a dark mirror.

The great trees hang over the water's face, their branches festooned with long strands of Spanish moss, a grey lichen-like plant that looks like innumerable grey threads hanging from the trees. Then there are orchids in hundreds of different shades, which grow on the trunks and the branches, sometimes in such quantities that the trees seem as though studded with jewels.

Generally, as I say, the waterways are like long lanes of polished mirrors, but occasionally, growing on the surface of the water, you will come across a thick mat of green water plants from which tiny flowers of mauve and yellow thrust up their petals a few millimetres above the surface. In sunny spots near the bank, you will see great clusters of the giant water-lily, whose flowers are bigger than a teapot, and whose great plate-like leaves are the circumference of a bicycle wheel. When travelling up one of these overgrown creeks in a boat, it is as though you are sliding over a green lawn, for, as you move along, the nose of the boat thrusts the water-plants aside and, passing on, the plants float together again so that no water is visible. With the movement of the boat, ripples cause the water-plants to rise and fall in green waves in your wake.

When we arrived in Guiana, our base camp was in the capital of Georgetown. For here it was easy to obtain a large and regular supply of food for our animals, and we could be within easy reach of the docks, when we had to load the collection on to the ship. Having made our base camp, we would then take trips into the interior of Guiana, visiting the different types of country and capturing the animals that lived there.

The first trip of this sort that I made was to the grasslands near the Pomeroon River. We set off from Georgetown and headed up the creeks in the direction of a small Amerindian town called Santa Maria, hidden away in the depths of this strange, swampy country. It took us a whole day to reach our destination and it was an unforgettable trip. As the boat slid smoothly up the polished waterways under the brilliant trees, big black woodpeckers with scarlet-crested heads flew ahead of us, giving wild shrill cries and stopping every now and then on a dead tree to rattle on it vigorously with their beaks. In the undergrowth along the bank were flocks of marsh birds, the size of a sparrow, with black bodies and brilliant canary-yellow heads. Occasionally, as we rounded a corner, a pair of scarlet ibis would fly up in a flutter of pink and crimson wings.

On the aquatic vegetation along the edge of the creek there were great numbers of jacanas, a strange-looking bird rather like an English moorhen. The most astonishing thing about them is that they have long, slender legs ending in a bunch of great thin toes. These toes enable them to walk over the water-plants on the surface of the water without falling through, for with each step the jacana spreads out its toes like a spider and distributes its weight evenly over the lily leaves. When they are walking solemnly across the lily pads they look rather drab little birds, but when they fly you can see that they have a brilliant lemon yellow patch under each wing.

Occasionally, we would disturb a cayman lying on the bank. This is the South American equivalent of the crocodile in Africa. They would watch us for a moment with raised heads, their mouths half open, and then would scuttle heavily to the edge of the bank and plop into the water.

We arrived at Santa Maria late that night, and the next day, with the help of the Amerindian villagers, set out to collect our animals. Many of the Amerindian people keep the wild forest animals as pets and a number of these they allowed us to buy, so in a very short time we acquired a great number of brilliant macaws, whose screams and shouts nearly deafened us in our small hut, several young boa-constrictors and two or three Capuchin monkeys.

I was very surprised to find the Amerindians keeping boa-constrictors as pets, for I had expected to find them as frightened of snakes as the Africans were. Inquiring about it, I discovered that they kept these reptiles in their huts crawling about on the rafters, and they took the place of the domestic cat in England. Feeding on any rats or mice they came across, these snakes would become very tame and, as long as the supply of rats and mice lasted, remained up in the rafters and never ventured down to the ground. The Amerindians explained to me that not only were the boa-constrictors far better rat catchers than any cat, but they were handsome pink, silver, black, and white creatures which were considerably more beautiful than cats to look at as they draped themselves like coloured scarves in the roofs of the huts.

In Guiana there are found three different kinds of ant-eater. There is the giant, which with its great shaggy tail, measures over six feet in length, there is the tamandua which is about the size of a pekinese, and there is the pygmy which only measures about eight inches long. Now these three ant-eaters live in completely different types of country and, although they are occasionally found in each other's territory, they mainly stick to the country which suits them best. The giant ant-eater prefers to live on the grasslands in the northern half of Guiana, while the other two, being arboreal, inhabit the forested regions. The tamandua can be found even in the semi-cultivated portions of the country, but to find the pygmy, you have to go into the deep virgin forest.

To capture a giant ant-eater for our collection, I had to fly some two hundred miles inland up to the northern grass fields or savanna-land. The plane dropped me off at a remote ranch on the banks of the Rupununi River. Here I enlisted the aid of an extremely clever Indian hunter who was called Francis. I explained to him what I wanted, and after a lot of thought he said the best way would be for him to go out into the grass fields and search about until he found signs of where a giant ant-eater was living. Then we could go out and search for the animal and try to capture it.

I agreed to this plan, and three days later Francis turned up at the ranch-house, beaming all over his face, to tell me that he had been successful. Somewhere in a certain patch of the savanna, he had found unmistakable signs of an ant-eater's presence, in the shape of ants' nests that had been split open by its powerful claws.

So, very early Francis and my friend and I, mounted on horseback, set off after the ant-eater. The golden grass fields, dotted here and there with small clumps of tiny shrubs, shimmered in the rays of the sun and stretched away in every direction to the distant horizon where there was a rim of pale greeny-blue mountains. We rode for hours and saw no life at all except a pair of tiny hawks circling high in the blue sky above us.

Now I knew that the grasslands had their fair share of animal life and I was rather surprised that on our ride we did not come across more creatures. I soon discovered why this was, for as we were riding along, we came to a great oval hollow in the bottom of which was a placid lake filled with water-lilies and fringed with lush plants and small trees. In a flash, everything seemed to come to life. The air was full of zooming dragonflies, and brilliantly-coloured lizards scuttled about our horses' hooves; kingfishers perched on the dead branches of trees hanging over the water and in

Rhea

Crab-eating racoon

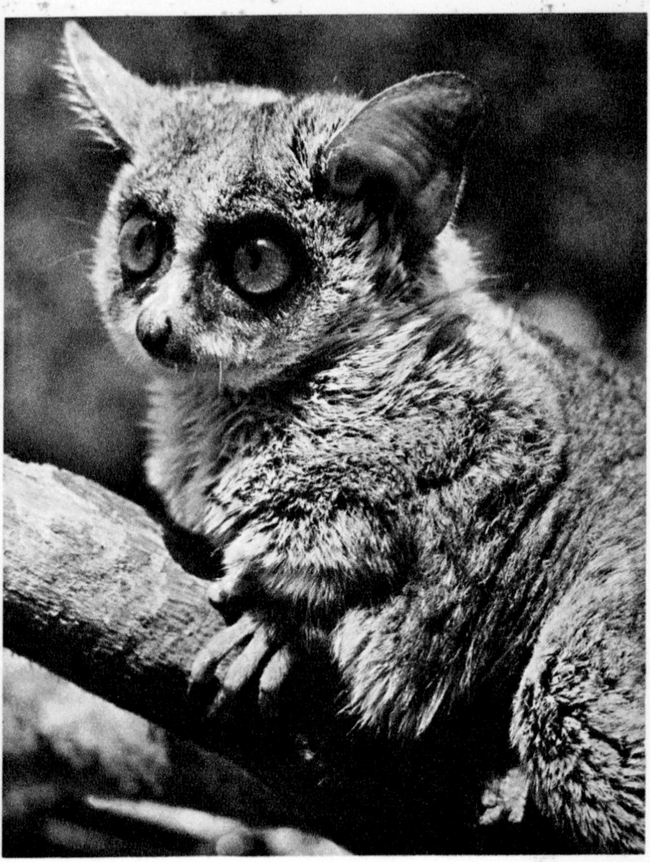

Bush baby

(a) Three-banded armadillo

(b) Capybara

(a) Horned toad

(b) Red river hog

Blackfooted mongoose

Tamandua

Douroucouli

the reeds and bushes alongside the lake there were hosts of tiny birds chattering and fluttering. As we rode past, I saw on the opposite bank ten jabiru storks, each standing about four feet high, and gazing down their long beaks with solemn expressions.

When we had passed the lake and once again entered the grass field, everything became lifeless again and the only sound was the steady crackle and swish of our horses' hooves in the long grass.

So I realized that the majority of these grasslands were waterless from the point of view of animal and bird life, and it was for this reason that they concentrated round the edges of the lakes and pools which were to be found. Therefore, you might ride for miles and see no life at all, and then you would come to a little hollow with a pond or lake in it and find that its shores were overflowing with bird and animal life.

Eventually, about midday, we reached our destination, a certain spot in the savanna, at which Francis halted his horse and told us it was in this area that the ant-eater was living. He said it would be best for us to spread out in a line and ride through the long grass, making as much noise as possible so as to frighten the ant-eater out of its sleeping-hollow. We could then drive it on to an area of savanna with short grass, which lay to our left, and we could overtake the animal more easily on horseback. We plunged into the long grass which was as high as our horses' chests and made our way shouting and creating as much noise as possible.

The earth under the grass was baked as hard as a brick by the sun and split with great cracks and holes, so our horses often stumbled and almost threw us over their heads. Suddenly, I heard a loud yell from

Francis, and looking towards him I saw a dark shape hopping about in the grass just ahead of his horse. My companion and I turned our mounts and rode down to help our hunter. The ant-eater, for that was what I presumed it to be, was trying to get still deeper into the long grass but we managed to cut him off and drive him out on to the open patch of ground. He galloped along, his thick stubby legs thumping the

ground, his long icicle-shaped head swinging from side to side and his great tail fluttering out behind him like a banner.

We rode after him as quickly as possible and I went to one side to prevent him from getting back into the long grass while Francis took the other side, uncoiling his lasso as he urged his horse on. Gradually he drew level with the galloping ant-eater, and whirling his lasso he threw it. He had, unfortunately, made a mistake in the size of the noose. It was too big and so, although it was well in front of the ant-eater, the animal just simply galloped through it and continued on across the grass, snorting and hissing. Francis halted his horse, re-coiled the rope and set off in pursuit once again. He drew level with the animal and threw his lasso again. This time he was lucky, and drew the rope tight round the ant-eater's neck.

He was off his horse in a moment, hanging on grimly to the end of the rope while the angry ant-eater rushed on across the grass, dragging him with it. I jumped off my horse and ran over and laid hold of the rope as well. It was quite amazing the strength the ant-eater had in his stubby legs for he dragged us to and fro across the savanna until we began to feel quite exhausted and our hands were being cut by the rope. Francis, looking over his shoulder, grunted with relief. Looking round, too, I saw that our struggle had brought us fairly close to a small tree about twelve feet high. This was, in fact, the only tree to be seen for miles.

Sweating and panting we dragged the reluctant ant-eater towards this, and then wound the loose end of the rope round and round the tree trunk and tied it fast. I had just tied the last knot when Francis glanced up into the branches of the tree above and gave a yelp of dismay. Looking up, I saw about two feet above our heads a large circular wasps' nest about the size of a football. The ant-eater, tugging on the end of his rope, was making the tree sway and bend, and the wasp colony was not at all pleased with this and they were swarming out on the outside of the nest, buzzing angrily. Francis and I retreated with all speed.

Now that we had the ant-eater safely tied up (or so

we thought) we went back to the horses to collect the various items that we had brought with us – some strong twine and some large sacks for carrying the quarry in. When I returned to the tree I was just in time to see the ant-eater claw off the last loop of rope, shake himself like a big dog, and start off plodding across the savanna in a slow and dignified manner. Leaving Francis to retrieve his lasso from the wasp-infested tree, I ran after the ant-eater on foot, fashioning a slip knot at the end of a length of twine as I ran.

I rush up to him and flung my amateur lasso at his head, but not being as skilful as Francis I naturally missed. The ant-eater kept plodding on; I tried again with equal lack of success and then a third time, but the ant-eater had become a litle irritated with my constantly flinging yards of twine at him and he suddenly stopped, faced round, and rose up on his hind legs. In this attitude his head was on a level with my chest and I looked warily at the great curved six-inch claws on his front feet that he held at the ready.

He snuffled and sniffed, waving his long, slender snout from side to side and swinging his forearms so that he looked rather like a boxer. As I did not fancy having a rough and tumble with a creature that was obviously capable of doing considerable damage with his front claws, I decided that it would be better to wait until Francis had joined me and then one of us could attract the animal's attention, while the other tried to capture him. I walked round the ant-eater to see if I could take him unawares, in the rear, but he merely revolved like a top, always keeping his big claws pointed menacingly at me. So I sat on the ground to wait for Francis.

The ant-eater, realizing that there was a break in

hostilities, decided that it would be a good chance for him to repair the damage done to his person by his fight with us. As he had run about the savanna, hissing and snorting, great streams of saliva had been pouring out of his mouth. This was thick and sticky, and normally the ant-eater uses it for coating his long tongue, in order to pick up his food. However, these long strands of adhesive saliva had run out of his mouth; as he ran they flapped to and fro picking up bits of stick and grass and eventually getting stuck across his nose. He now sat on his haunches and with great care cleaned his long snout with the aid of his claws. Then he gave a deep sigh, stood up and shook himself, and started to plod off across the savanna once more.

When Francis joined me, carrying his lasso, we approached the ant-eater once again, and hearing us he stopped, turned round, and sat up on his hind legs, but with two of us to deal with he was at a disadvantage. While I attracted his attention, Francis crept round behind and threw the lasso neatly over him. As soon as he felt the noose tighten once more round him he set off at full tilt, dragging Francis and myself with him, and for the next half an hour we struggled our way to and fro over the savanna until we managed to get so many loops of rope round the ant-eater's body and legs that he could not move. Then trussing him up with an extra length of fine twine to make sure, we pushed him into one of the big sacks so that only his long head and nose protruded.

We were just congratulating ourselves on having captured him when a fresh difficulty became apparent. When we picked him up in his sack and carried him towards the horses they all decided that, while they did not mind carrying us, they disapproved strongly of carrying a strange creature in a sack, which was hissing and snuffling in such a fierce manner. For a quarter of an hour we tried to soothe them, but it was no good. Every time we approached them with the ant-eater they would throw back their heads and shy wildly.

Francis decided that the only thing to do was for me to lead the horse while he walked behind, carrying the ant-eater on his shoulders. I was a bit doubtful as to whether this would be successful, for we were a great many miles from the ranch and the sun was scorchingly hot, and the ant-eater was no light-weight. However, it seemed to be the only thing to do, so I mounted on my horse and led Francis's, while he staggered along behind with our capture on his back. The ant-eater made everything as difficult as possible by wriggling about in his sack, so that it was extremely uncomfortable to try to carry him. After about an hour we had only progressed a couple of miles across the grass, for every two or three hundred yards Francis was forced to put down the sack and have a rest.

Eventually, we decided that it would take us about a week to get the ant-eater back to the ranch at this rate, so Francis suggested that my companion, or myself, should remain there with the ant-eater while the other rode with him to the out-station, a distant speck on the horizon which he pointed out to us. Here, he assured us, we would get something called a 'draftball'. As our hunter's English was none too good, we could not make out what a 'draftball' was, but Francis seemed convinced that it was the only way out of our difficulties, so my companion stayed with the ant-eater in the shade of a small bush while Francis and I galloped off across the grass towards the out-station.

When we arrived there, we found a charming old Indian in charge who gave us a most welcome cup of coffee. Then Francis took me outside and showed me the 'draftball'. It was in fact a draught bull, that is to say, a bull that is used for carrying loads or pulling carts in certain parts of the world.

Francis's wife then appeared on the scene and Francis told me that she would ride the bull out on to the savanna while we galloped on ahead on our horses. This tiny Indian woman jumped up on to the enormous bull's back and sat there side-saddle, her long black hair hanging down to her waist, so that she looked rather like Lady Godiva. Then she gave the bull a whack on the rump with a large stick and he set off at a brisk trot over the grasslands.

When Francis and I arrived back at the place where we had left my friend and the ant-eater, we found that the ant-eater had succeeded in making things difficult for us. He had managed to climb half-way out of his sack, which was now hanging round his hind quarters like a pair of rather baggy trousers, and he was scuttling to and fro across the grass hotly pursued by my friend. We caught and pushed him into a new sack and tied him up even more securely, while my friend recounted the difficulties he had undergone during our absence.

Apparently, first of all his horse, which we thought was securely tied up, had suddenly wandered off across the grass and my friend had pursued it for quite a long time before he managed to catch it. When he got back, he found the ant-eater had succeeded in wriggling free of some of his cords and had ripped open the sack with his claws and was half out of it. My friend, frightened that he might escape, rushed forward, pushed him back into the sack and tied him up once again. When he looked round he found that his horse had seized the opportunity to wander away once more.

By the time he had captured his mount and returned to the ant-eater, the beast had broken out of his sack for the second time. It was just at this point that we had arrived back on the scene.

Presently, Francis's wife galloped up on the bull's back and she helped us to load the ant-eater on to it. The bull was very quiet about the whole business and did not seem to mind whether the sack on his back was full of potatoes or rattlesnakes, and although the ant-eater hissed and struggled as much as he could, the bull plodded steadily onwards, taking not the slightest notice.

We reached the ranch just after dark and there got our capture out of the sack and untied him. I made a rough harness out of the rope and tethered him to a big tree; also, a large bowl of water was placed there for him and he was left to have a good night's sleep.

Very early the next morning I crept out to have a look at him, and at first glance I thought he had managed to escape in the night, for I could not see him. I realized after a while that he was lying between the roots of the tree, curled up in a tight ball, and had spread his tail over himself, like a great grey shawl, so that from a distance he looked less like an ant-eater and more like a pile of old cinders. It was then that I realized how very useful his big tail must be to him. In the grasslands he scrapes himself a shallow bed in among the big tussocks of grass, curls himself up in this and spreads his tail over himself like a roof, and only the very worst weather could succeed in penetrating this hairy cover.

My problem now was to teach Amos, as we called him, to eat a substitute food, for he could not be fed on a diet of white ants at the zoo in England. The mixture was composed of milk, raw egg, and finely minced beef, to which was added three drops of cod-liver oil. I filled a large bowl with this mixture and took it along to a big white ants' nest, which was not far from the ranch-house, and, making a hole in the nest, collected a handful of the creatures and scattered them over the surface of the milky substance in the bowl. I carried the whole lot back and placed it where Amos could reach it.

I thought it would be some time before he would take to this new food, but, to my surprise, on seeing the bowl, he rose to his feet and ambled forwards. He sniffed carefully and flipped out his long snake-like tongue and dipped it into the mixture. Then he paused for a moment, musing over the taste, and having decided that it was to his liking he stood over the bowl, his long tongue flipping out and in with amazing rapidity until it had been licked quite clean. The ant-eaters, of course, have no teeth and rely on their tongues and the sticky saliva to pick up their food.

Occasionally, as a special treat, I would give Amos a bowlful of termites which were, naturally, all mixed up with lumps of their clay nest. It was amazing to watch his long tongue come out and dip into the pot so that the white ants and the bits of clay stuck to it like flies to a flypaper. But then as he drew his tongue back into his mouth again, the bits of clay would be knocked off by his lips, so that only the white ants were sucked inside. He was really extremely clever at doing this.

Not long after I arrived back at our base camp in Georgetown, and Amos had settled down in his new pen, I succeeded in getting a wife for him. She arrived one day tied up in a snorting bundle and crammed into the boot of a taxi-cab. The person who had captured her had not been very careful about the job and she had several nasty cuts on her body and was extremely exhausted through lack of food and water. When I took the ropes off her, she just lay on her side on the ground, hissing in a very feeble manner, and I did not think that she was going to live. I gave her a bowl of water to drink, and no sooner had she sucked it up than she revived most miraculously and got to her feet and started attacking everyone in sight.

Amos had got used to being the only ant-eater in the place and did not receive his mate very kindly. When I opened the door of his pen and tried to push the female inside with him, he gave her a loving greeting by bashing her on the nose with his claws and hissing furiously. Eventually I decided that they had better share adjoining cages until they had got used to one another. Amos's pen was very large, so I just simply divided it down the middle with stakes. Now, whereas Amos had been no trouble at all about his food, his new wife was extremely difficult. She refused point-blank even to sample the mixture that I gave her in a bowl, and for twenty-four hours she was on this hunger strike.

The day after her arrival, however, I had an idea. When I was feeding Amos, I pushed his bowl close to the wooden bars that separated him from the female. Amos's table manners were not of the very best, and anyone standing within thirty feet of him, when he was having his food, was made well aware of the fact, even if they could not see him, by the sucking, snorting, and snuffling sounds that he produced. The female ant-eater, attracted by the noises of Amos enjoying his breakfast, went over to the bars to see what it was he was eating. She stuck her slender nose between the stakes and sniffed at his bowl of food, and then very slowly and cautiously she dipped her long tongue into the mixture. Within a couple of minutes she was gobbling it down with the same speed and enthusiasm that Amos displayed. And for the next fortnight, she ate all her food like this, with her neck stuck through the bars and her long tongue sharing the bowl with Amos.

At last, by constantly feeding out of the same pot, they became quite used to each other and it was not long before we removed the bars in between and allowed them to share the pen. They became very affectionate and would always sleep close together, their tails carefully spread over themselves. For the voyage home, however, I could not get a cage big enough to hold the two of them, so they had to travel in separate boxes. When we were on board ship, however, I pushed the two cages close together, so they could stick their long noses out and sniff at each other.

When they eventually arrived back in England and went off to the zoo, they used to amuse crowds of visitors by giving boxing matches. They would stand up on their hind legs, their great noses swinging from side to side like pendulums, clouting and slashing at each other with their long, murderous-looking claws, their tails swishing and sweeping on the ground.

These boxing matches looked fast and furious, but never once did they hurt each other.

The second biggest ant-eater found in Guiana is the forest-loving tamandua. This looks not unlike the giant; it has the same long curved snout and small beady eyes and the powerful front feet with great hooked claws. It is clad in short, light-brown fur and

its tail is long and curved. Whereas the giant ant-eater uses its tail as a form of covering, the tamandua cannot do this with his, but he uses it as the tree porcupine or the monkeys in Guiana use theirs, to assist him in climbing up trees. The tamanduas were the most stupid creatures we ever caught in Guiana.

In the wild state they clamber up the tall forest trees and work their way out along the great branches until they find a large earth nest of the tree ants. Using their great hooked claws, they break open the ant fortress and proceed to lick up the ants with their long sticky tongue. Every now and then they will break off a little more of the ants' nest and go on with their licking. In captivity they find it difficult to rid themselves of this habit and when you present them with a pot of minced meat, raw egg, and milk, they dip their long claws into it, lick up a bit and then scrape at it again with their claws. It would usually end with them overturning the pot on the floor of their cage. They were under the impression that the pot was a sort of ants' nest that had to be broken in order to get at the contents, and it was only by fixing their food dish to the wire that I could prevent them from splashing their food all over themselves and the cage.

The first of the pygmy ant-eaters that I obtained was in an Amerindian village in the creek islands. I had been travelling all day by canoe, visiting various settlements and buying whatever animals they had for sale. In this particular village I found quite a good haul of pets and spent an entertaining hour or so bargaining with the villagers. As they could not speak English and I could not speak their language, it all had to be done in sign language.

Presently, through the thick of people surrounding me, a small boy of about seven or eight years of age pushed his way, carrying in one hand a long stick, on the end of which was something that at first glance I thought was a giant chrysalis of one of the big forest butterflies. However, on looking more closely I discovered that it was a pygmy ant-eater, clinging to the branch with its eyes tightly closed. I bought it off the boy and found that there were a lot of interesting points about the little animal which I had not seen mentioned in any book on natural history.

The little creatures measure about six inches long and are completely clad in thick soft golden-brown fur, that makes them look more like tiny toy teddy bears. Their long, prehensile tail is also thickly covered. The soles of their hind feet, which are bright pink in colour, are slightly cupped, so that when the creatures scramble about the branches their feet fit round the twigs and give the ant-eater an excellent

grip. When a pygmy ant-eater is holding on with his hind feet and his tail, it is almost impossible to pull it off the branch without seriously hurting it. Like its relatives, its forefeet are short and very powerful and are armed with three curved claws, a big one in the centre and two small ones on each side. The palm of its paw is like a small pink cushion and, when it grips with its front feet, the long claws snap down on to the palm with tremendous strength, rather like a blade of a pocket-knife fitting into the slot.

These little animals have a very curious habit which has earned them the name among the natives of Guiana of 'Tank 'e God'. When asleep, the creature sits clasping the branch with its hind feet and tail wound round tightly, sitting upright like a guardsman, with its two front paws raised heavenwards. If it is disturbed in any way, it will fall forwards on its enemy and the two large claws on its front paws will slash and rip its assailant. The ant-eater will also adopt this odd position when it is frightened, and will squat there for sometimes as long as half an hour, its paws raised high above its head, its eyes closed, waiting for an opportunity to attack.

The little ant-eater was extremely slow and sleepy in his movements and seemed so resigned to his capture that I did not even have to put him in a box, but just leant the twig he was sitting on in the bows of the canoe, and he stood there very stiffly and upright, like a figurehead on an old ship, and remained without moving until we reached our camp. I was not at all sure what sort of food the little fellow would eat, but I knew from books that this tiny animal lives on the nectar of various forest flowers. So the first evening, I mixed up a solution of honey and water, and hung a little pot of it in the ant-eater's cage.

About eight o'clock that evening, he started to show signs of life. He got down from his stiff, upright attitude and started to crawl in among the branches in his cage in a slow and cautious manner: he was like an old man on a slippery road. Then he discovered the pot of honey. He was hanging on the bars just below it and he sniffed it very carefully with his short pink nose and then decided that it probably contained something worth eating. Before I could stop him, he had hooked a claw over the edge of the little dish and tipped it up, and the next moment he was covered in a shower of honey and water. He was extremely indignant about this, and even more irritated when I had to take him out of the cage and mop him up with a piece of cotton-wool; for the rest of the evening he sat on a branch, cleaning off the sticky remains from his fur.

He enjoyed honey and water very much, but I had to give it to him in a pot with a very small mouth, otherwise he would dip his whole head into it and then climb down on to the floor and wander about, so that by the time morning came, he looked like a moving ball of sticky sawdust.

Honey and water, however, did not give the little animal sufficient nourishment, and so I tried him on some ants' eggs. To my surprise, he firmly refused to eat these; then I tried him with the ants themselves, and he appeared to be even less interested in them than he was in their eggs. Eventually, more by mistake than anything else, I discovered that he liked grasshoppers and moths, and he would pursue these round his cage with great vigour every evening.

The ant-eaters of Guiana are certainly not the easiest of animals to keep in captivity, but they are very fascinating beasts and it is well worth taking some trouble over them.

CHAPTER TEN

Toads that have pockets, and other weird beasts

THE creeks ran all round the village of Santa Maria, and so to all intents and purposes we were living on an island. The creeks, I found, were full of vast numbers of baby caymans, and I was very anxious to catch a good supply of these. I soon found out that it was not quite as simple as had been the capturing of crocodiles in the Cameroons. For there you wade along the shallow streams and catch them on the sandbanks. The creeks round Santa Maria were far too deep to do this, quite apart from the fact that they were inhabited by other things besides caymans, such as electric eels and a vicious and bloodthirsty fish called the piranha, both of which would make unpleasant bathing companions. So, in order to capture the baby caymans, I had to adapt my method for hunting crocodile to the country I was in.

We had a big canoe and went off down the creeks late one night, taking with us a big torch and a long stick with a cord tied to the end, which terminated in a slip-knot. I sat right up in the bows of the canoe, holding the torch and this stick, while the paddler in the stern propelled us slowly and gently across the dark waters. I soon found that the baby caymans preferred to lie in the places where the weeds were thick on the surface, with just their noses and their bulbous eyes sticking out. As we moved gently along

I shone the torch to and fro over these patches of weed, until eventually I saw the fiery glow of a baby cayman's eyes some thirty yards away. Using my free hand to signal, I guided the paddler in the stern until we came to the edge of this weed patch and then signalled him to slow down and eventually stop.

Keeping the beam directed into the creature's eyes, I leant forward, slipped the noose of cord gently over his head, and then, with a quick jerk, pulled him right out of the water and into the boat, where he wriggled

and uttered loud indignant snoring grunts. As soon as they heard these protests, all the other baby caymans for miles around started grunting in sympathy, but this proved to be their undoing, for by listening to the direction from which the grunts came, I could tell where the greatest number of them were hiding, and it was not long before I had a bulging sack on the floor of the canoe which wriggled and slithered as the reptiles moved inside. This great quantity of caymans made such a noise that we could not progress any farther, for everything for miles around could hear the canoe coming with all the baby caymans grunting in unison.

One of the strangest inhabitants of this watery world of the creeks was the pipa toad. It is probably one of the most extraordinary amphibians in the world, for it is quite literally a toad with pockets. I caught some of these strange creatures in a small leaf-choked channel leading off one of the big main creeks. They were so very like the messy decomposed leaves that at first sight I did not recognize them as anything living. They measure about five inches long and look rather like very flat leathery brown kites with a leg at each corner. They did not spit and struggle when I picked them up, as most toads and frogs would do, but lay quite limply relying on their resemblance to the dead leaves to protect them.

One of the specimens I caught was a female with eggs, and I was particularly pleased with this, as it gave me a chance to watch the astonishing hatching of the baby toads. When the female lays her eggs, the male presses them into the skin on her back which has grown soft and spongy in order to receive them. So at first sight they look like transparent beads half buried in the brown leathery skin. Gradually the half of the egg that is above the skin hardens and forms little convex lids, so the eggs remain in the mother's back in this series of pockets and slowly change into tadpoles and then into tiny toads, each one so small that it would take six of them to cover a postage stamp. When the baby toads are ready to hatch, the edge of the eggshell sticking above the skin becomes soft, and, by wriggling and pushing, the little creatures manage to push the lids back, like trapdoors, and then by much exertion they manage to haul themselves out of their strange potholes – like nurseries in their mother's back.

This big female that I caught in the creek lands spent her time in a big tin can, lying on the surface of the water, quite still, and looking as though she had not only been dead several days, but as though decomposition had already set in. Gradually, I watched the eggs on her back harden into little lids, and then I waited patiently for the baby toads to make their

appearance. In actual fact, they put off their entry into the world until I was on the homeward voyage and half-way across the Atlantic, when they chose the most awkward time to appear.

It was about midnight, just when I had finished the work and was thinking of retiring to my cabin, that I glanced at the female pipa toad, before switching out the light in the hold, and saw a strange little black twig which appeared to be growing out of her back. On looking closer, I discovered that one of the small lids had been pushed away and this black object was the tiny arm of a baby toad sticking out of his nursery and waving to and fro. As I watched, he managed to get the other arm out and then his head, when he paused for a moment and looked for all the world like a tiny black workman coming out of a manhole in a road.

It took him about four or five minutes to get right out of his nursery and he lay there for some time on her back, apparently exhausted by his efforts. Then he slid off and plopped into the water, where he started to swim around merrily. I waited there patiently, and presently another of the tiny lids was pushed back and a second baby toad started to wave his arm at me.

As I was squatting there, absorbed and fascinated by this extraordinary sight, I was joined by two sailors who, coming down from their watch on the bridge, had seen the light on in the hold and had wondered if there was anything the matter and, if so, whether they could help. They were rather surprised to find me crouching over a tin at that hour of the night and asked what I was doing. I explained the history of the big female pipa toad and how we had caught her in the mysterious creek lands and how, now, the babies were busily hatching out of her back. The two sailors squatted down beside me and watched the arrival of yet another baby toad, and soon they became as fascinated as I.

Presently, the three of us were joined by yet more sailors who had wondered what had happened to their companions. Once more, I told them the tale of the toad with pockets and they too became so intrigued that they sat down to watch the hatching of the toads. When one baby, more weak than the others, took an extra long time to get out of his pocket, the sailors grew very worried and wanted to know if they could help him with the aid of a matchstick, but I explained that the baby toad was so fragile that the matchstick would appear to him like a tree trunk, and however gently we tried a manoeuvre it, it was more than likely to break one of his thread-like arms or legs.

Eventually, when this baby hoisted its toes out of the pocket and fell in an exhausted heap on his mother's back, there was a general sigh of relief. Dawn had broken before the last of the toads plopped into the water, and we rose from our cramped positions and went down into the kitchens of the ship to see if we could beg an early-morning cup of tea from the cook. But in spite of the fact that we all yawned over our work that day, we agreed it had been well worth sitting up all night to watch the arrival of the baby toads.

The pipa toads were not, of course, the only unusual amphibians to be found in the creek lands. Guiana seemed to have more than its fair share of unusual toads and frogs.

Next to the pipa toads I think the strangest we caught was the paradoxical frog. We first came across evidence of this creature late one night when my friend and I were dredging a small stream to see what we could catch. Presently, my friend called to me and said that he had caught the strangest creature: it looked just like a tadpole, except that it was about six inches long, with a body about the same size as a hen's egg.

My friend and I had a long argument as to what this peculiar beast could be; he insisted that it must be some kind of fish, as if it were a tadpole it would grow into a giant frog. I was just as certain that it must be a tadpole. It was only after we had argued for some time that I suddenly remembered having read about this weird amphibian, and then I knew that the creature we had captured was the tadpole of the paradoxical frog.

The paradoxical frog's life history works in the opposite way to an ordinary frog. With a common frog the spawn hatches out into tiny tadpoles, and these grow until, on attaining a certain size, they develop legs, their tail is absorbed, and they crawl out on to dry land as a medium-sized frog. This is one of the most extraordinary things in the world, for the paradoxical frog is bigger when it is a baby than when it is fully grown.

Another curious frog found in this part of South America is the pouched frog. This little beast cares for its young in almost as unusual a way as the pipa toad. The female pouched frog has a long slit in the skin of her back that opens into a sort of pocket; into this the eggs are placed, and the female more or less forgets about them. Inside the pocket the eggs change into tadpoles, the tadpoles grow legs and their tails are absorbed, and when they are ready for the world, the mother thereupon splits the skin down her back, and out pop the babies, each not much larger than the knob on the top of a knitting-needle.

One of the smallest but most powerful amphibians caught by us in Guiana was the poison arrow frog. These are small tree frogs, each measuring perhaps an inch and a half long, and decked out in the most wonderful colours and patterns. There are several species, and they might be red and gold striped on a cream background, or pink and blue on a black background, or any other combination of colours. They are very lovely little things, and a jar full of them looks more like a mass of highly-coloured sweets than live creatures. To the Indian tribes these little frogs are most useful. They catch a number and put them close to a fire. As soon as the frogs start to become hot they exude a kind of slime from their bodies, which the Indians scrape off and collect. This slime, prepared in a special way, is a most potent poison, and the Indians use it to dip the tips of their arrows in. Thus, when the arrow strikes an animal – even a quite powerful one, like a wild pig – the poison works very rapidly and kills the beast. So, for the Indians, each of these little tree-frogs is a miniature poison factory in itself, and whenever they need fresh material for their arrows they go off into the forest and collect a number of the frogs from which to manufacture it.

CHAPTER ELEVEN

In which Cuthbert the curassow causes trouble

ONE of the most charming but irritating specimens that I got in Guiana was Cuthbert the curassow. I bought him when I was up in the creeklands, and he started being a nuisance almost immediately. The curassow are large birds, as big as a turkey, with jet black feathers all over their bodies, bright yellow feet and a thick yellow beak. The feathers on the top of their heads stand up and curl forwards in a short crest, and they have large, dark eyes with a mad expression in them.

Cuthbert arrived, being carried by his owner, who was a fat and shy little Chinaman. When I purchased the bird, the Chinaman stooped and placed him on the ground near my feet. He stood there for a minute or two blinking his eyes and uttering a soft plaintive 'peet-peet-peet', a noise which was amazing, coming from such a large and fierce-looking bird. I bent down and started to scratch his curly crest and immediately Cuthbert closed his eyes and fell flat on the ground, shaking his wings with delight and giving a sort of throaty crooning noise.

The Chinaman assured me that he was very tame and that I did not need to shut him up in a cage, as he would not wander away. Since Cuthbert seemed to have taken such a fancy to me I decided that this was probably correct. When I left off scratching his head, however, he rose to his feet and walked closely beside my legs, still peeting ridiculously. Very slowly he crept forward until he was close enough, and then he lay down across my shoes, closed his eyes, and started to croon again. He was gentle and so sloppy in his character that there and then I decided to call him Cuthbert, as I felt that this was the only name that really suited him.

On the evening of Cuthbert's arrival, I was sitting at a small table in our hut, endeavouring to write up my diary, when Cuthbert, who had been wandering thoughtfully about the room, decided that it was time he bestowed a little affection on me. So he flew up on to the table with a great flapping of wings and walked across it, peeting in a pleased tone, and tried to lie down across the paper on which I was writing. I pushed him away irritably, and as he stepped backwards, with a look of outraged astonishment on his face at such treatment, one of his great chicken-like feet upset the ink, which, needless to say, went all over the diary, so that I had to rewrite two pages of it.

While I was doing this, Cuthbert made several attempts to climb into my lap but I warned him off vigorously, and eventually he wandered away and stood in deep thought for a few minutes. He decided that approaching me in this slow manner was not successful and so he would have to try and take me by surprise. He waited until I was not looking and then took off and tried to fly up on to my shoulder. He missed his mark, of course, and crashed on to the table with outstretched wings, uttering a shrill squawk of dismay, and upsetting the ink for a second time. I left him in no doubt as to how angry I was and so he retreated into a corner of the room and sat there sulking.

Presently my companion came into the hut, in order to perform the nightly task of hanging up the hammocks in which we slept. He pulled them out of the corner where they were stacked, and was busily occu-

pied in disentangling them from their ropes when Cuthbert spotted him and decided that if I would not pay any attention to him, perhaps my companion would. He cautiously crept across the room and then lay down just behind my friend's feet and closed his eyes.

While my friend was struggling with the ropes and hammocks, he stepped backwards suddenly and tripped over the bird behind him. Cuthbert gave a squawk of alarm and retired to his corner once more. When he thought my friend's attention was fully occupied, he came out, crept up to him and lay down across his shoes for the second time. The next thing I knew, there was a crash and my companion fell to the floor, together with all the hammocks, and from beneath the tangled mass of mosquito nets, rope, and canvas, Cuthbert's head peered out, peeting with great indignation at such unmannerly treatment. I made up my mind that he had caused quite enough trouble for one evening, so I took him over to the part of the hut where I kept the animals and tied him with a long cord round his leg to a heavy box and left him there, peeting away vigorously to himself.

Late that night, when we were asleep in our hammocks, I was woken by a terrific uproar coming from the direction of the animals' cages. I jumped out of my hammock and, seizing the small lantern which I always kept by my bed for such emergencies, dashed over to see what was happening. I found Cuthbert sitting on the floor, looking extremely annoyed and peeting away to himself. Apparently, he had looked round the various cages and decided that the only one that would be suitable for him to roost on was the cage inhabited by a group of small squirrel monkeys. So he had flown up on top and prepared himself for sleep. Unfortunately, he did not notice that his tail was dangling down in front of the bars and in the bright moonlight the monkeys could see it quite clearly. They were very intrigued by it, and so they pushed their hands out through the bars to feel it and find out what it was. When Cuthbert felt them lay hold of his tail, he obviously thought that he was being attacked by some monstrous animal and flew up to the ceiling like a rocket, leaving two of his large tail feathers still firmly gripped in the monkeys' paws. It took me a long time to soothe his ruffled feelings and to fix him up a new place to sleep, on which he felt quite safe from attack from the rear.

When Cuthbert eventually arrived back at our base camp in Georgetown, I let him have the run of the

big garden in which I kept the animals, and he was always creating an uproar, owing to his delight in collapsing across people's feet when they were not looking. The garden was surrounded by a very tall fence made of corrugated iron which was too high for Cuthbert to fly over.

However, he became convinced that if he went on trying hard enough he would eventually succeed in getting over the top of the fence. So every day he used to practise. He would walk away ten yards and then turn round, run towards the fence with a fierce expression on his face, flapping his wings so that gradually his heavy body would rise from the ground and he would zoom towards the fence, flapping vigorously.

But he never quite succeeded in getting high enough and he had never mastered the art of being able to turn suddenly in mid-air, and so he would fly on and on, straight for the fence, and as it came closer and closer and it became quite obvious to him that he was going to crash into it, so he would utter loud squawks as if he were endeavouring to tell the fence to get out of the way. Then there would be a terrible crash and Cuthbert would slide down the corrugated iron in a flurry of feathers, his long nails making the most blood-curdling screeching noises as he tried to stop himself. These crashes that he had did not seem to do him or the fence any harm, and as long as he was happy, I left him alone.

One day, however, Cuthbert approached the fence to have his daily battle with it and discovered to his delight that someone had left a ladder leaning up against it. By the time I had noticed this, Cuthbert had hopped his way up to the top rung and was sitting there looking extremely proud of himself. As I went up to the ladder to try to catch him, he flapped his wings and flew down on to the road on the other side. There he stopped for a moment to have a quick preen before sauntering off in the direction of the market. Hastily I called all our helpers and we rushed out into the road in pursuit of the truant Cuthbert. He glanced over his shoulder and saw us bearing down on him in a body, and so he turned and ran as fast as he could.

He led us a gay dance round the market-place with half the stall owners and most of the customers joining in the hunt, and it was not until half an hour later that we eventually cornered him and carried him peeting loudly back to the garden.

Other birds that used to cause us a lot of amusement were the big highly-coloured macaws. All these birds had been hand-reared by various people in Guiana, from whom I had purchased them. So they were all quite tame. For some reason or other all macaws in Guiana are called Robert, in the same way that parrots in England are generally called Polly, so when you bought a macaw you were quite certain that, as well as being able to scream like a factory siren, they would be able to say their own name. We had eight of these birds and they would carry on lengthy and most amusing conversations with each other, using only the word 'Robert'. 'Robert?' one would say in a questioning tone of voice. 'Robert, Robert, Robert,' another one would reply. 'R-r-r-robert,' a third one would say, and so they would go on, and they would cock their heads on one side and look so wise that I was almost forced to believe that these silly conversations meant something.

One pair of these macaws did not like being confined in a cage at all, for they were used to having the run of the house. I used to let them wander all over the garden while we were in Georgetown, but when the time came for me to sail with the collection, I had to put the macaws in a cage. I built a very nice cage for them with a strong wire front but I had forgotten that with their great beaks these birds can gnaw their way through any sort of wood.

We had not been on the ship for more than three days before this pair of macaws had nibbled right round the edge of their cage front and the whole thing fell out with a crash. Three times I repaired the cage and pushed the angry macaws back inside it, and three times they nibbled my repairs to pieces and escaped once again. In the end I gave it up as a bad job and used to let them wander round the hold whenever they wished. They would walk slowly and carefully along the tops of the line of cages, talking to me or to their companions in their 'Robert' language.

CHAPTER TWELVE

In which I meet several new animals including the moonshine unwarie

---

ONE of the most amusing animals to be found in Guiana is the tree porcupine. It is a short, fat creature covered with black and white spines, and has a long, naked tail which it uses to aid itself in climbing trees. It has fat, flat hind feet, a great swollen wobbling nose and two small round eyes like bulbous boot buttons. If these funny-looking creatures had not been so absurd to watch, you would have felt quite sorry for them, for they did everything with a well-meaning, rather puzzled air, and they were always very surprised when it turned out to be the wrong thing.

If four bananas were given to one of them, for example, he would first of all try to carry all the fruit in his mouth. When, after several attempts, he had come to the conclusion that his mouth was not big enough to accommodate this quantity, he would sit there with his bulbous nose whiffling about, wondering what to do. He would pick up one banana and hold it in his mouth, and then clasp one in each paw but then, looking down, he would discover to his dismay that there was still one left on the ground, so he would drop the one he had in his mouth and pick up the one that was left on the ground. Then he would notice that there was still one banana to be carried, so he would put the whole lot down again and sit and think about it. Eventually, after about half an hour's struggle, a brilliant idea would strike him, and sitting there he would eat one of the bananas and carry off the other three triumphantly.

These porcupines had an amazing habit of indulging in boxing matches. Two of them would climb into the upper branches of their cage and settle themselves

comfortably on their haunches, facing each other, twisting their strong tails around the branches for extra safety. Then they would lunge and parry at each other with their paws, aiming savage upper-cuts and short-arm jabs to the body, while all the time their noses whiffled from side to side and their little round eyes had a meek and rather worried expression in them. The amazing thing about these boxing matches was that they would go on sometimes for as long as half an hour, but never once during the whole of that time did one porcupine hit the other one.

Sometimes, after their bout of sparring, they would do a little juggling. They would find an old mango seed, or something similar, and, sitting on their haunches, would toss it from paw to paw in a fumbling sort of way that made you think they were about to drop it at any moment, but they never did. Watching them, I was very much reminded of the sad, flat-footed, mournful-faced clowns you see at the circus, who are for ever getting into trouble, or doing something funny with the most serious expressions on their faces.

Guiana can boast of having, among other strange creatures, the largest rodent in the world, a creature called the capybara. These look rather like gigantic guinea-pigs, grow to the size of a large dog and can weigh nearly a hundredweight. They measure about four feet long and stand about two feet high at the shoulder. Compare this with the English harvest-mouse which measures four-and-a-half inches including its tail and weighs about one-sixth of an ounce. Seeing these two animals together, you would never believe they were related.

I got my first capybara very soon after our arrival

in Georgetown; in fact it was, I learned, *too* soon. I had not yet found a suitable spot for our base camp and we were living in a small boarding house in the back streets of the town while I searched. Our landlady very kindly said that we might keep any animals that arrived in her garden until such time as I moved our base camp.

Very soon I had a bird and one or two monkeys in neat cages piled up near her flower beds. Then, one evening, a man walked in leading on a length of string a fully-grown capybara. While I bargained with him, the capybara wandered about the garden with a fearfully aristocratic expression on his face, occasionally nibbling at a bloom when he thought I was not looking.

Eventually, I bought the rodent and put him in a large, new cage that I had built, which was long and coffin-shaped with a specially strong wire front. All sorts of delicacies were piled in for him to eat and he was left to settle down. The room in which I slept overlooked the garden, and at about midnight my companion and I were woken by a most peculiar noise. It sounded like someone playing a Jew's harp, accompanied by somebody else banging in a vague sort of way on a tin can. I lay there, wondering what on earth it could be, when I suddenly remembered the capybara.

Uttering a loud cry of 'The capybara's escaping!' I leapt out of bed and rushed downstairs into the garden in my pyjamas, where I was soon joined by my friend.

In the garden everything was quite quiet and we found our rodent sitting on his haunches, looking down his nose in a superior manner. My friend and I had a long argument as to whether or not it was this animal that had been making the noise. He insisted that it could not have been, because, he said, the capybara looked so innocent, and I said that it was the capybara for exactly that reason. Since the sound was not repeated, we went back to bed, and no sooner had we settled down, than the awful row started again,

only this time it was worse than ever. Looking out of the window I could see the capybara's cage shaking and shuddering in the moonlight.

Creeping downstairs and approaching very cautiously, we could see what the animal was doing. He was sitting there in his cage with a rather sneering expression on his face; then he leant forward and put his great curved teeth round a strand of the wire front, pulled hard and released it so suddenly that the whole cage vibrated like a harp. He waited until the noise had died away and then raised his fat behind and thumped with his feet on the tin tray, crashing away like thunder. I presumed he was applauding his own musical efforts. We decided that he was not trying to escape but merely doing this because he liked the sound it produced.

It was out of the question to allow him to continue making this noise, for I felt that before very long the other people in the boarding-house would start to complain. So the tin tray was removed and the front of the cage covered with sacking in the hope that this would soothe him into going to sleep. Then, hopefully, we went up to bed again. No sooner had I snuggled down than, to my dismay, the awful twanging sound started once more in the garden. I could think of nothing with which to put a stop to it, and while my friend and I were arguing about it, several of the other people in the house woke up and came along to knock on the door and tell me that one of the animals was escaping and making so much noise in the process that they had been awakened. I apologized profusely to them while wondering what on earth could be done to stop the wretched rodent.

It was my friend who had the bright idea: he suggested that we carried the capybara, cage and all, down to the natural history museum, which was not far away and with whose curator we were friendly; the beast could be left there in charge of the night-watchman; and we could collect him on the following morning. We put our clothes on over our pyjamas and, going down into the garden, crept up to the long, coffin-shaped cage, wrapped it in sacks, and started off down the road with it. The capybara was very annoyed at having his private concert disturbed and showed his disapproval by running from one end of the cage to the other, making it tilt up and down like a see-saw. It was only a short way to the museum, but because of the capybara's antics we had to rest several times.

We rounded the last corner to the museum gates and bumped straight into a policeman. It is extremely difficult to explain to a policeman why you are carrying a large rodent in a cage through the streets of the town at one o'clock in the morning, especially when you have dressed hurriedly and bits of your pyjamas are hanging out of your clothes. At first, I think, the policeman thought we were burglars just back from a raid on some nearby house, then he decided we must be murderers who were carrying the corpse of our victim in this coffin-shaped box. Our story about the capybara he obviously found very difficult to believe and it was not until we had unwrapped the sacks and shown him the animal that he realized we were telling the truth.

He then became very charming, and even helped us to carry the cage up to the museum gates, and there the three of us stood and shouted for the night-watchman, while our captive, in order to soothe our ruffled feelings, played us a little tune on the wire cage front. But there was no response to our shouting and it was soon obvious that the night-watchman, wherever he might be, was certainly not watching the museum. After thinking about things for a bit, the policeman suggested we should take the capybara down to the local slaughterhouse where there was sure to be a night-watchman who would probably take care of the beast until the morning.

On the way to the slaughterhouse we had to pass our boarding-house once again and I, therefore, suggested that we left the animal and his cage in the garden until we had been to the slaughterhouse and made sure they would give him a night's lodging. It was quite a long way and I did not think it was very sensible to carry him there only to find they would not accept him.

So leaving the capybara still inventing little songs on his cage front, we wended our way sleepily through the empty streets, and eventually, after losing ourselves once or twice, found the slaughterhouse, and to our joy there was a light in the window. We threw stones up at it and called until presently a very old Negro poked his head out and inquired as to what we wanted. I asked if it would be possible for him to give a night's lodging to a capybara, but he obviously decided that we were both quite mad, especially when we said that we had not brought the animal with us but would go to fetch it, if he would take it in. Then he wanted to know what a capybara was, and when I explained that it was a large sort of rodent the old man looked very worried and shook his head.

'Dis place is slaughterhouse,' he said, 'dis place is for cowses. I don't tink rodents allowed here.'

In the end, however, I managed to persuade him that capybaras were really like 'cowses', only smaller, and it would not ruin the slaughterhouse to keep the creature for me for one night. With that settled, we walked back to our boarding-house to fetch the beast. There, the moonlit garden was silent and serene, and, on looking into the cage, we saw the culprit curled up in the corner asleep, snoring gently to himself. So we left him, and he slumbered on and did not awaken that night. We came down the next morning, feeling quite exhausted after our nocturnal efforts to obtain a temporary abode for the animal, to find the capybara looking very fit and not the slightest bit tired.

There are found in Guiana several species of animals called opossums, which are chiefly remarkable for the fact that they are the only animals outside Australia which carry their young as a kangaroo does, in a pouch. The opossums in South America all look rather like rats with long, shaggy fur and long, naked tails, though the different species vary in size, some being as big as a cat and others as small as the smallest mouse. As I say, they look very rat-like; it is when you see them climbing about in the trees that you realize they are really nothing like rats at all. Not only can they climb as skilfully as monkeys, using their hands and feet, but they can also use their tail to help them as well, and it twists and turns its way around the branches like a snake: indeed, its grip is so strong that, even if they should lose their hold with their hands and feet, they could hang suspended by their tail and save themselves from falling to the ground.

The most attractive of the Guianese opossums was one of the smaller varieties. The people in Guiana call the opossums 'unwaries', and this particular kind they called the 'moonshine unwarie', because they said it only came out when the moon was full. They were really quite pretty little animals with dark charcoal-black upper parts; a lemon-yellow tummy; pink tail, feet, and ears; and two thick, white eyebrows of fur, similar to coloured bananas over their dark eyes. They were about the size of an ordinary rat, although their faces were much more pointed and their tails much longer.

The first moonshine unwarie I obtained was

brought to me by a little East Indian boy who had caught it in his garden late one night. He came with the animal dangling on the end of a piece of string just as I was about to leave that particular village to travel back to our base camp in Georgetown. The ferry-boat was waiting to take me down the river, and I really had not a moment to lose.

Half-way down the road towards the quay I remembered that I had no cage on board the ferry in which to house the little opossum. So I decided that I had better return to the shop in the village and buy a box which could be made into a cage on our journey down river. My companion ran ahead to hold up the ferry-boat until I arrived; and so, carrying the irritated little animal dangling on the end of his string, I rushed madly back down the road to the village shop and breathlessly asked the man behind the counter if he could let me have a box.

He tipped out a whole lot of tins on the floor and silently handed me the box in which they had been. Grasping it in my hand and gasping out a word of thanks I dashed back along the road. The little East Indian boy accompanied me, and as we ran he took the box from my hands and carried it skilfully on his head. Running down the dusty road in the hot sun was very exhausting, and each time I paused for breath I could hear a loud, peevish hoot from the river ferry, which would spur me on, and at last I reached the quay just as their patience was exhausted and they were about to remove the gangway.

On board the boat, and after recovering my breath, I set about preparing a cage for my opossum, and when this was ready I had the unpleasant task of untying the string round the animal's waist. By this time it was not in a very good temper and hissed at me like a snake and bit savagely at my fingers, but I succeeded in cutting the cord. As I did so, I noticed a strange sausage-shaped swelling in the skin of its stomach between its hind legs. I thought it possible that the little animal had been damaged internally. While I was gently feeling this peculiar lump, however, my fingers parted the fur and I found myself looking into a long shallow pocket in the opossum's skin in which were four minute quivering pink babies.

This was the reason for the strange swelling, and not some injury that she had received. The mother was very indignant at my looking at her pouch without permission, and she screamed loudly and snapped at me. When I put her into the cage, the first thing she did was to sit up on her hind legs, open her pouch, and make sure that all the babies were there. Then she combed her fur into place and set about eating the fruit with which I had provided her.

As the four babies grew larger, they soon found it a very tight fit inside that shallow pouch, and it was not long before only one of them would fit in it at a time. They would lie around on the floor of the cage near their mother, but if anything frightened them, round they would turn and dash towards her in a mad race, for they knew that the one to get there first was the only one that could crawl into the shelter of her pouch, and the others would have to stay outside and face whatever danger threatened. When she was moving about the cage, the mother opossum would make all her babies climb on to her back, where they would cling tightly to her fur and twine their slender pink tails around their mother in a firm and loving embrace.

CHAPTER THIRTEEN

In which I catch a fish with four eyes

WHEN I was in Guiana, I was very anxious to obtain some of the beautiful kinds of humming-birds which are to be found there. After some time, I happened to contact a hunter who was particularly good at catching these minute birds, and about once a fortnight he would bring me a small cage with five or six inside, fluttering their wings so rapidly that it sounded more like a cageful of bees. I had always been told that humming-birds were extremely difficult to look after, and was, therefore, very worried about the first four I acquired.

In the wild state they feed on the nectar from flowers, hovering in front of the blooms and sticking their long, fine beaks inside, lapping up the substance with their fragile tongues. In captivity they have to be taught to drink a mixture of honey and water with a small amount of Bovril and some Mellin's food mixed with it. This mixture, in the heat of the tropics, goes sour very quickly, and for this reason the humming-birds have to be fed three times a day. The job was, of course, to teach them to feed out of a little glass pot, for they were used to getting their meals from a highly-coloured flower, and did not realize at first that the pots contained the nourishment they needed.

When they first arrived, I removed each one very carefully from the cage and, holding it in my hand, dipped its beak into a pot of honey and water, time and time again, until eventually it stuck its tongue out, tasted the mixture and then began to suck it up greedily. When it had had a good feed, I put it in its new cage with one of the pots of food inside, and then plucked a scarlet hibiscus flower and placed it inside the pot on the surface of the honey.

The humming bird, which was about the size of a bumble-bee, sat on its perch and preened itself and uttered tiny little chirrups in a self-satisfied sort of way. Then it took off from the perch and purred round and round the cage like a helicopter, its wings

moving so fast that they were just simply a dim blur over its back. Eventually, as it was flying around, it caught sight of the hibiscus flower lying in the pot, and swooped down and pushed its beak towards the bloom. When it had sucked all the nectar out of the flower, it continued stabbing with its beak and soon stuck it between the petals and into the honey beneath, and started to drink rapidly, still hovering in mid-air.

Within twenty-four hours it had learnt by this means that the little glass pot hung on the wall of its cage contained a copious supply of the sweet honey, and from then onwards I did not have to bother to give it a sign-post in the shape of a flower.

These tiny birds settled down very happily, and in two days they had become so tame that when I put my hand inside the cage with the pot of food, they would not wait for me to hang it on the wire but would fly down and drink it as I was putting it in, occasionally perching on my fingers for a rest and to preen their glittering feathers.

There was generally something exciting happening at our base camp in Georgetown. You never knew at what hour of the day or night someone would arrive with some new specimens. It might be a man carrying a monkey on his shoulder or a little boy with a wicker cage full of birds, or it might be one of the professional hunters turning up after a week's journeying into the interior, with a large horse-drawn cart piled high with cages full of different creatures.

I remember one day a very old Indian walked into the garden, carrying a raffia basket which he handed to me very courteously. I asked him what was inside it and he told me that it contained rats. Well now, it is perfectly safe to take the lid off a basketful of rats, as, generally, they will simply crouch on the bottom and not attempt to move. I removed the lid of the basket and found that it was not full of rats but full of marmosets, who leapt out with great speed and agility and fled in all directions. After a hectic chase that lasted about half an hour we managed to round them all up and get them into a cage. But it taught me to be

more cautious about opening baskets full of specimens that were brought in.

These little marmosets were about the size of a rat with a long, bushy tail and intelligent little black faces. Their fur was a deep black colour and their paws were a bright orange-red. We kept them in a large cage where they had plenty of room to scuttle about, and gave them a box with a hole in it to act as their bedroom.

Every evening they would all come down and sit by the door, chattering and squeaking, waiting for their supper. They would drink a potful of milk and then have five grasshoppers each, and, after crunching up the very last morsel, off they would troop in a line, the oldest one leading, and solemnly climb into their box and all curl up in a solid ball at the bottom. How they were able to sleep like this without suffocating, I have no idea, but apparently marmosets sleep in colonies in the wild state as well as in captivity.

One day, a tall Negro walked into the garden and trotting alongside him on a long string was a most extraordinary-looking animal. It was similar to a gigantic guinea-pig covered with great white blotches. It had large dark eyes and a mass of white whiskers. It was, in fact, a paca and a near relation of the guinea-pig and also of the capybara. When we had agreed on the price that I was to pay for this animal, I asked the Negro if it was tame, whereupon he picked it up, stroked it and talked to it and assured me that he had had it since it was a tiny baby, and that a more gentle creature you could not wish to find. At that particular time I had received a large consignment of animals and was, therefore, short of cages. But since the paca was tame, I thought I would simply just tie him up to a nearby stump. I did this and gave him some vegetables to eat, and promptly forgot all about him.

Some time later I was walking down the line of cages, taking out the water pots to wash them, when quite suddenly I heard a snarl that would have done credit to a tiger, and something flung itself at my leg and buried its teeth in my shin. Needless to say, I leapt in the air and dropped all the water pots which

I had been so carefully collecting. It was, of course, the paca which had attacked me, though why he should have done so I cannot imagine, for he seemed perfectly tame when he arrived. My trousers were torn and my leg was bleeding. I was extremely angry with the animal, and for the next week he was quite unapproachable; if anything went near him he would dash at them, gnashing his teeth and uttering his ferocious snarling grunt. Just as suddenly as his bad temper had flared up, and for no apparent reason, so he became tame all over again and would allow you to scratch him behind the ears and tickle his tummy while he lay on his side. His behaviour alternated in this manner all the time he was with me, and whenever I approached his cage it was with the uncertainty of not knowing whether he was going to greet me with signs of affection or a savage bite from his large sharp teeth.

One of the most extraordinary specimens that we were brought while in Georgetown, was a small fish, some four or five inches long. A dear old Negress came to us one day with about five of them in an old tin kettle. When I bought them, I tipped them out into a large bowl, and I realized at once that there was something peculiar about them, but for a few seconds I could not place what it was. Then suddenly I noticed that there was something very strange about the fish's eyes. I took one out of the bowl and put it in a glass jar, so that I could examine it more conveniently, and then I saw what it was that had puzzled me: the fish had four eyes.

Its eyes were large, and situated so that they bulged above the surface of its head, rather like a hippo's eyes. Each eyeball was neatly divided into two, with one eye on top of the other. I discovered that this fish spends its life swimming along the surface of the sea, so one set of eyes looks downwards and keeps a watch for any large fish that may make an attack, while the other pair keep a look-out along the surface of the water for food, and above in case of attack by a fish-eating bird. It was certainly one of the most amazing defences I have ever seen in an animal, and certainly one of the most extraordinary fishes.

Guiana seems to go in for amazing forms of life. There, one of the most peculiar birds in the world is to be found, the hoatzin, or, as it is called in Guianese, the Stinking Anna, because of its strong musky scent. This strange bird has a 'thumb' on its wing, armed with a hooked claw. A baby hoatzin, a few hours after hatching, can scramble out of its nest, and crawl about in the trees like a monkey, using its thumb to get a grip on the twigs. The nests are built in thorn-bushes overhanging water, and a few hours after hatching, the babies think nothing, if any danger threatens, of dropping ten feet into the water where they swim and dive like fish. When the danger has passed, they use their thumbs to climb the tree and get back into the nest. The hoatzin is the only bird in the world able to do this, and the babies make a weird sight swinging among the thorns, or plopping into the water like little men clad in furry bathing-suits.

CHAPTER FOURTEEN

Which describes the giant cayman and the shocking electric eel

---

KEEPING my animals in Georgetown was very good from a number of points of view: it was an excellent source from which to obtain food for my collection and also, by going down to the market, some nice new specimens brought in by traders from outlying districts could be picked up. There, too, I was also within fairly easy reach of the airport, and this meant that consignments of delicate creatures could be sent off regularly to England by air. The creatures that travel best by aeroplane are the reptiles, and so every two weeks or so I would pack up several big boxes full of a mixed assortment of frogs, toads, tortoises, lizards, and snakes, and get them driven down to the airport.

Sending reptiles by air is very different from sending them by sea. To begin with, they are packed in another way. To send off, say, a consignment of snakes, you need a large, light wooden box; you place each snake in a small cotton bag, tying up the opening firmly with string; then, drive nails into the sides of the crate and hang the bags from these. In this way, you do not have to worry if one kind of snake is going to eat another, for they are all separated and yet can be sent in the same box. The air trip from Guiana took about three days, and all the snakes had to have during that time was water, for these reptiles can go for long periods without food, and come to no harm. My snakes were given a good feed the day before their departure, and they would lie curled up in the little cotton bags, digesting the meal; by the time they had finished it, England would have been reached.

Frogs and toads and the smaller lizards were also sent in bags, and much the same rules applied to them. But for the larger lizards, such as the green iguana, special crates are necessary, and into each one you would put five or six iguanas and give them a lot of branches, wedged inside the box, so that they would have a plentiful supply of footholds on which to cling. Baby caymans, I found, travel very successfully by air, but the bigger ones did not take to it at all, and, quite apart from this, they weighed so heavy in their wooden crates that the freight charges were enormous: so most of the big caymans came back with me on board the ship.

The smallest cayman I caught in Guiana measured a little over six inches in length, and he must have been quite newly hatched. The largest one measured over twelve feet and was not nearly so tractable to deal with. He was caught in a big river up in the northern savannas, a river full of enormous electric eels and hundreds of caymans. Upon hearing that a zoo in England wanted a particularly large cayman, I decided that this was the spot to try to catch one. Just below the place where I was staying, the river had hollowed out a small bay in the bank, and opposite to this bay, about a hundred and fifty yards away, was an island, and it was there that these creatures spent their time.

The trap that I used to catch them in was very primitive but most effective: two long, heavy native canoes were pulled up on to the little beach of the bay, so that they were half-way out of the water and about a yard apart from each other, leaving a channel between them: in this channel I fitted up a noose attached to a bent sapling. Also attached to the bent sapling was a big hook with a dead and extremely smelly fish on it. To get at the fish, the cayman would have to stick his head through the noose, and as soon as he attacked the fish the small sapling would be

released and, springing upwards, would draw the noose tightly round him. The other end of the rope was made fast to a big, strong tree on the bank some six feet above. I set my trap late one evening, but thought it very unlikely to make a catch much before the next day.

That night, just before going to bed, I felt it might be a good idea to go down and make sure that the trap was still set and ready, and, my friend joining me, we walked together down to the river bank, through the dark strip of woodland. Drawing near to the place where the trap was set, we could hear the most peculiar noise, a dull thudding sound, but could not make out what it might be. On reaching the bank, though, we soon saw what was causing it. An enormous cayman had crawled up the channel between the two boats, and, just as I had hoped, had stuck his head through the noose and pulled at the fish, and the rope had fastened tightly round his neck. Looking over the bank and shining our torches downwards, we could see the gigantic reptile writhing and splashing between the two boats which he had pushed far apart in his struggles.

His great mouth was opening and closing with a thud, like a chopper on a block, and his thick tail was lashing from side to side, churning the waters to foam, and thumping against the sides of the two boats, so that it was a wonder he had not smashed them in. The rope round his neck was fastened to a tree on the top of the bank, near where we were standing, and it was stretched taut, and each time his great weight pulled on it we could hear it humming with the strain. The tree itself was shaking and quivering with the cayman's efforts to free himself, and continued to shudder when the cayman unexpectedly lay still in the foaming water, as if he had exhausted himself; and then I did an extremely silly thing.

Leaning over the bank, I took hold of the rope with both hands and started to haul it towards me. As soon as he felt the movement on the rope, the cayman renewed his efforts with the utmost vigour. The rope twanged taut again, and I found myself jerked over the edge of the cliff, to hang there more or less in mid air with my toes on the extreme edge and my hands grabbing the rope. I realized that if I let go and fell, it would mean crashing straight down on to the reptile's scaly back, where, if not bitten by his huge jaws, I would most certainly be brained by a blow from his mightily muscular tail. All I could do was to cling on to the rope, and presently my companion managed to lay hold of it too. This enabled me to get a foothold on the bank and haul myself back to safety, and we both let go of the rope.

At once, the cayman lay still again, and we decided that the best thing to do would be to return to the house and collect more rope to tie him up with, since we felt that if we left him all night with just that one rope round his neck, he would eventually, in his struggles, break it and escape. We hastened back and collected all the things we needed Then, carrying two lanterns and several torches, we went again to the river. The cayman was lying still, blinking up at us with his large eyes, each of which was the size of a walnut. The first thing to do was to put his great toothed jaws out of action, and for that purpose a noose was gently lowered, flipped over his snout, pulled tight, and fastened to the tree. While my companion held the lights, I crawled down into one of the boats, and after a certain amount of trouble, managed to get another noose over the cayman's tail and work it down to the very base near the hind legs, where I worked it tight. This rope was also fastened to the tree. Thus, having three ropes on him, and feeling that the cayman was reasonably safe to be left, we retired to bed.

The next morning, together with some natives, we went down to the river and began to work out a plan for getting the huge reptile out of the water and up the steep bank to the top, where he could be picked up by a jeep. The natives had brought along with them a long, thick plank, and this we tried to slide under the reptile so that he would be lying lengthways upon it. However, he was in such shallow water that we could not manoeuvre the plank under him, for his belly was buried in the mud. The only thing to do was to loosen the rope and float him out a yard or two into deeper water where we could push the plank under him with greater ease. This we did, and bound him to the plank with coil after coil of rope round his nose, his tail and his short powerful legs.

The next job was to get him out of the water and up the bank. It took twelve of us an hour and a half to accomplish this, for we were working on sticky clay, and every time we managed to haul the great bulk of the cayman up a few inches, we would have to pause and then, to our dismay, he would slide back again to his original position. It was hard work, but we succeeded in pushing him right up to the top of the cliff and over on to the short, green grass where we surrounded him, covered with clay from head to foot and dripping wet, and very pleased with ourselves.

Another river creature which created quite a spot of bother was the electric eel. This occurred when I was collecting down in the creek lands. My friend and I had been out all day in a big canoe, paddling up and down the remote waterways, visiting various Amerindian villages and buying whatever pets they had for sale. We bought, among other things, a tame tree porcupine and, at the last village, had discovered a wicker basket containing a half-grown electric eel. This, too, I bought and was very pleased at the addition to my collection, since it was the first of these creatures that I had obtained.

We settled ourselves in the canoe and started homewards, tired but pleased at having had such a successful day. I was sitting up in the bows with the tree porcupine curled up asleep between my feet. Farther along, in the bows, was the electric eel wriggling hopefully round and round in his wicker basket. Beside me sat my companion and behind him the two paddlers in the stern of our rather unsafe craft.

My attention was first drawn to the escape of the eel by the tree porcupine who, in a complete panic, endeavoured to climb up my leg and would, if allowed, have continued right up to my head. Wondering what on earth was the matter, I handed him to my companion while I had a look round in the bows of the canoe to see what had frightened him. Peering down I saw the electric eel coming towards my feet in a very determined manner. It gave me such a fright that I jumped straight up in the air and the eel passed under me, and I landed once more in the canoe, fortunately without overturning it.

The creature meanwhile wriggled towards my friend. I shouted to him to watch out, and he, holding the porcupine in his arms, tried to stand up and get out of its way, failed, and fell flat on his back in the bottom of the canoe. The electric eel slid past my friend's struggling body and headed for the first paddler. He, too, when faced with the eel, was no braver than we; he dropped his paddle and prepared to abandon ship.

The situation was saved by the very last occupant, the second paddler. He was apparently quite used to finding electric eels in canoes in mid-stream, for he simply leant forward and pinned the creature to the bottom of the craft with his paddle. I threw him the basket, and with a few quick movements he had managed to scoop the eel back inside it.

We all felt very relieved and even started to make

jokes about it. The rescuer handed the basket with the eel in it to his fellow paddler, who in turn, handed it to my friend. As he was about to pass it to me, the bottom fell out and the eel was once more among us. This time, luckily, it fell draped over the side of the canoe like a croquet hoop. It gave a quick, convulsive wriggle, there was a splash, and our electric eel had disappeared into the dark waters of the creek.

It was a disappointing end to what had been an exciting quarter of an hour, but later on we were able to obtain several more of these creatures, so we did not regret its loss. A big electric eel is capable of producing quite a considerable amount of current, and has been known to kill even horses and men while they were crossing rivers in various parts of South America. The organs for producing the electricity are situated along each side of the creature's body; in fact, almost its entire length is a gigantic battery.

The eel swims along, looking rather like a large, thick black snake, and when it suddenly comes upon a fish it stops short, its whole body seems to shudder, and you see the fish twitch and curl up and then float gently down, either paralysed or completely dead, while the eel darts forward and sucks it into his mouth whole and always head first. Sinking to the bottom of the creek, he will lie there meditating for a few minutes, and then shoot upwards, stick his nose above the water and take a lungful of air before continuing his search for another victim.

PART THREE

Perambulations in Paraguay

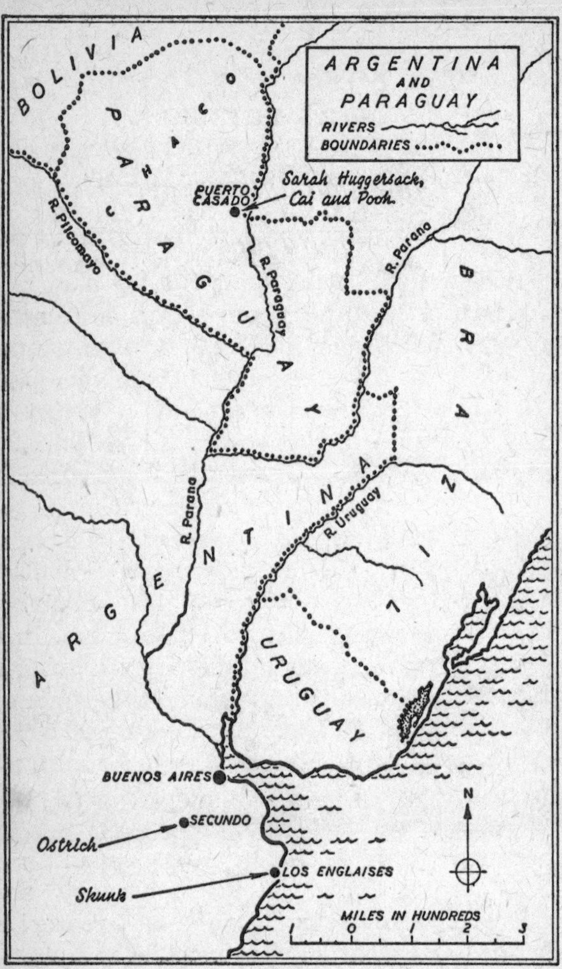
ARGENTINA AND PARAGUAY
RIVERS
BOUNDARIES
BOLIVIA
CHACO
PARAGUAY
ARGENTINA
BRAZIL
URUGUAY
PUERTO CASADO
Sarah Huggersack, Cai and Pooh
R. Pilcomayo
R. Paraguay
R. Parana
R. Parana
R. Uruguay
BUENOS AIRES
SECUNDO
Ostrich
LOS ENGLAISES
Skunk
N
MILES IN HUNDREDS
1 0 1 2 3

CHAPTER FIFTEEN

In which I hunt with the gauchos

NOW I should like to tell you about my most recent collecting trip. I returned recently from a six months' expedition to the Argentine and Paraguay. Argentina is a country that has an absolutely fascinating animal life, totally different from that found anywhere else in South America. As nearly the whole country is composed of the vast grasslands called the pampas, naturally all the creatures are adapted to life on these open plains. The pampas in the Argentine are remarkably flat; standing at one point, you can see the great grassland stretching away as smooth as a billiard table until it mingles with the sky on the horizon. In the long grass grow the giant thistles that resemble the English thistle, except in size. Here they grow to a height of six to seven feet, and to see large areas of the pampas covered with them in bloom is a wonderful sight, the green grass appearing to be covered with a sort of purple mist.

Hunting for animals in this open grassland is not quite as easy as it might at first appear. To begin with, most of them live in holes and only venture out at night. Secondly, there is very little cover in the way of bushes or trees, and so the quarry can generally spot the hunter some way off. Even if he does not, he will probably be warned by the spur-winged plover who, from the collector's point of view, is quite the most irritating bird of the pampas. They are very handsome-looking, somewhat like the English plover with their black and white plumage, and are always seen in pairs. They have remarkably good eyesight and are extremely suspicious, so that when anything unusual comes within their range, they rise off the ground and wheel round and round, giving the shrill warning cry of *tero . . . tero . . . tero,* which puts every animal for miles around on its guard.

One of the commonest creatures found in these great grassy areas is the hairy armadillo. These animals live in burrows which they dig for themselves, and which may extend anything up to thirty or forty feet beneath the surface; and, when they venture forth at night, if anything disturbs or alarms them, they make a bee-line for their burrows and dive down to safety. Naturally, the best time to hunt for them is at night, and preferably a night when there is little or no moon. We would go out from the ranch-house, in which we were staying, and ride our horses to a suitably remote spot. From then on we would go on foot, armed with torches, following the two hunting dogs who were experts in finding these little beasts. You have to be able to run very fast when hunting armadillos, for the dogs generally scamper off some distance ahead, zig-zagging about with their noses to the ground. As soon as they find one, they give tongue, and the quarry is off, racing back to the safety of his burrow. If this is close by, there is little chance of catching him. On our first night out hunting armadillos, we managed to catch some other members of the pampas fauna at the same time.

We had walked about two miles, wending our way

carefully among the giant thistles, which could prick like the spikes of a porcupine if brushing too close to them, when, suddenly, the dogs could be heard barking ahead of us and we all broke into a run, scrambling and jumping over the tussocks of grass and dodging in and out of the thistles. It was so dark that on more than one occasion I ran straight into a clump of thistles, and so by the time I reached the

place where the dogs were sniffing around their quarry, I was thoroughly pricked all over. The dogs were clustered at a respectable distance around something in the grass, and upon switching on our torches we saw, standing there very defiantly, a creature about the size of a cat, neatly clad in black and white fur, and with a handsome black and white bushy tail that stuck up straight in the air: it was a white-backed skunk.

He watched us without the slightest trace of nervousness, obviously convinced that he was more than a match for us and the dogs. He would occasionally utter a little sniff and then give two or three small bounds towards us, bouncing on his front feet. If we ventured too close, he would turn round and present his bottom to us, peering over his shoulder in a warning manner.

The dogs, who were well aware that the skunk would spray them with his powerful, foul-smelling scent, had kept a discreet distance from him, but while the creature was showing off to us, one of the dogs, rather unwisely, seized the opportunity to rush in and try to bite him. The skunk jumped straight up into the air and, in the same movement, wheeled round, so that his back was towards the dog, and the next minute the dog was rolling over and over in the grass, whining and rubbing his face with his paws, while the cold night air was filled with the most pungent and disgusting odour imaginable. Even though we were some distance away, it made us reel back, coughing and gasping, with the tears running down our cheeks, rather as though we had taken a deep sniff at a bottle of ammonia.

After this exhibition of his powers, the skunk trotted towards the dogs and gave one or two little skips in their direction that sent them all scuttling out of his way. Then he turned about and did the same thing to us, and we scuttled just as fast as the dogs had done. Having broken the circle around him, the little animal flicked his handsome tail up and down a couple of times and then sauntered off through the grass with an air of smug satisfaction.

We decided that we had no particular desire to get on more intimate terms with him, so we called the dogs and went on our way. The dog that had been squirted by the skunk continued to smell horribly for three to four days after this encounter, although the odour gradually wore off; but as we proceeded on our way the strong scent of the skunk, clinging to his coat, followed us through the night.

Catching skunks to keep in captivity is a difficult job. If their scent glands are left in, every time they are frightened they are liable to squirt everyone indiscriminately. These glands can be removed by a very simple operation, but this can only be done really successfully with a young specimen.

Some little time later, the barking of the dogs once more set us off on a wild scamper among the grass and

thistles, and now we found that our pack had discovered an armadillo who was scuttling along as fast as his short legs could carry him towards his burrow, while the dogs, yelping wildly with excitement, ran alongside, trying to bite his back, but making no impression on his armour-plated hide. He was easily captured, for we just simply ran up behind him, gripped him by the tail and hoisted him into the air, and we soon had him safely inside a sack. Greatly cheered with our first capture, we eagerly carried on, hoping to catch another one, but our next meeting was with a totally different creature.

We were close on the heels of the dogs, passing a small thicket of bushes, when a rather rat-shaped creature dashed out and disappeared among the thistles. The dogs set off in pursuit, and we were not far behind when we saw them catch up with the creature and snap at it, whereupon it fell down dead. The men called off the dogs and we approached the corpse. It proved to be a large opossum: an animal with a body about the size of a small cat, with a long rodent-like face. The body was covered with a brindled chocolate and cream coloured fur, the tail was long and resembled that of a rat, and the ears, like those of a miniature mule, were bare. When I complained to the men that the dogs had killed him, they all laughed uproariously and told me to look closer. Sure enough, when I shone my torch on him, I could see that he was still breathing, though doing it very quietly, so that it was almost imperceptible.

I found that I could move him about, even turn him upside down, and he still remained limp and, to all intents and purposes, as lifeless as could be, but in reality this was his method of defence, for he hoped that eventually, thinking him to be dead, we would go away and leave him to make good his escape. When we were putting our captive into a bag, however, he became alive to the fact that we had not been taken in by his trick, and wriggled and struggled, spitting through his open mouth like a cat and biting savagely at us. Later on we caught any number of these creatures and all of them, with the exception of the very young ones, who obviously hadn't yet learnt the trick of feigning death, tried to deceive us in exactly the same way.

On our way back to the ranch the dogs found yet

another hairy armadillo and, this time, I was treated to a display of the little animal's great strength. He was not far from his burrow when the dogs found him, and we were fairly close, but by the time we had caught up with him he had reached the mouth of his tunnel. One of the men flung himself forward in a magnificent flying tackle and caught hold of the armadillo's tail just as he disappeared into the earth. Another man and I threw ourselves, panting, alongside the first, and each of us grabbed one of the armadillo's hind legs. Now, only the forequarters of the beast were inside the tunnel, yet by digging his claws into the earth and by hunching his back and wedging it against the top of the burrow, he prevented the three of us from pulling him out, although we tugged and struggled as hard as we could.

It wasn't until the fourth member of our party arrived on the scene and with the aid of his hunting-knife cut away some of the turf that we were able to haul out the little creature. Then out he came, like a cork out of a bottle and with such suddenness that we all fell on our backs and lost our grip on him, so that he nearly made his escape the second time.

These two armadillos which we had caught very soon settled down and grew remarkably tame. I kept them in a cage which had a separate sleeping compartment; and they would spend the whole day lying there on their backs side by side, their jaws twitching, and uttering strangled snores. It was amazing how deeply they slept, for one could bang on the cage, shout at them, and even prod their pink, wrinkled tummies, and still they would lie there as if dead. The only way to rouse them was to rattle a food pan and, however gently this was done, they would both be wide awake and on their feet within the blinking of an eye.

All the species of armadillo in South America are used as food. I never had the opportunity of trying one, but I believe that when carefully roasted inside their shells – naturally after having been killed first – they taste like roast sucking-pig and are quite delicious. Many of the gauchos (South American equivalent of the North American cowboys) catch these little animals and keep them in barrels full of earth as a sort of larder, so that on special occasions they will be able to have roast armadillo.

As we were making our way home with our first captives, in the still night air I heard the distant sound of hoofbeats on the turf, gradually coming nearer and nearer, and then stopping suddenly within a few feet of us. It was rather a weird sensation, and I wondered for a moment if it might be the ghost of some old gaucho for ever galloping across the pampas. On asking my companions where the horse was that I thought I could hear, they all shrugged and in unison said 'Tucotuco.' It was then I realized what had caused the peculiar sound.

The tucotuco is a little animal about the size of a rat with a round, plump face and a short furry tail. He excavates enormous galleries just below the surface of the pampas and in these he lives, coming out only at night in search for the plants and roots on which he feeds. This strange little beast has very sensitive hearing, and when he catches the vibration of footsteps on the turf above his home, he gives out his warning sound, to let all the other tucotucos in the district know that there is danger about. How he produces this excellent imitation of a galloping horse is a mystery, but it may be his cry which, distorted by distance and echoes in his burrow, takes on the odd clopping quality of a galloping horse. Incidentally, tucotucos are very wary little beasts, and though we tried by many different methods to capture them, I was never successful in obtaining a specimen of this little creature which must be one of the commonest of the pampas fauna.

While we were staying in the Argentine, one of the things I particularly wanted to do was to make a cine-film of an old-fashioned gaucho hunt. The old style of gaucho hunting has nearly died out now, though many of the men still know how to do it. The animal, or bird, is pursued by men on horseback. Their weapons consist of the deadly boleadoras which are three balls attached to three lengths of string, all of which are joined together. These are whirled around the men's heads and then thrown. As they strike the quarry's legs, each ball on its cord swings round in a different direction, thus entangling the beast and bringing it to the ground.

There is a relative of the ostrich that lives in South America, called the rhea. It is not such a big bird as its African cousin, and its plumage is ash-grey instead of black and white, but the one thing that they both have in common is an ability to run extraordinarily fast. This bird used to be the chief quarry for this type of hunting in the days when rheas were found in vast flocks living on the pampas. On the ranch of a friend of mine there was still quite a large number of these birds living, and my friend offered to ask the gauchos if they would organize a rhea hunt, so that I could film it.

We set off early one morning; I in a small cart with a camera and other photographic apparatus, the gauchos riding on their magnificent horses. We made our way out across the pampas for some miles, weaving in and out of the thickets of the giant thistle. Presently, we disturbed a pair of spur-winged plovers who leapt into the air and flew around us, giving their alarm call, and, to our annoyance, warning every living creature for miles around of our approach. They accompanied us as we made our way forward, keeping an eye on us and keeping the pampas informed of our progress.

We had reached a large thicket of thistle plants when we were suddenly warned by ear-splitting cries from one of the gauchos that our quarry was at hand. Standing up in the cart, I could see a greyish shape dodging quickly among the thistles, and then, quite suddenly, the first rhea leapt out on to the open grass. He came bounding like a ballet dancer out of the thistles, stopped for one brief moment to look at us and then streaked off, his head and neck stretched out, his large feet almost touching his chin with each step. Quickly, one of the gauchos galloped out of the thistles and endeavoured to cut him off. The rhea seemed to stop in mid-stride, twirled round like a top and dashed off in the opposite direction, taking huge bounding strides, which made it look as though he were on springs.

He was very soon lost to sight, with the gauchos in hot pursuit. Before we had time to follow, another bird made its appearance out of the thistles. I could see this was a female, because she was much smaller than the previous one and a much lighter grey. To my surprise, she did not rush off in pursuit of her mate, but stood on the grass, dithering anxiously from one foot to the other. There was a crackling among the thistles and I saw the reason for her delayed flight. Out of the thistles scrambled her babies, ten of them, each standing about eighteen inches high and with round fat bodies, half the size of a football, balancing on thin stumpy legs and great splayed feet. They were covered with fluffy down and neatly striped with fawn and cream. They all clustered round their mother's feet, and she glanced at them lovingly. Then she trotted off across the pampas, running almost in slow motion, so that her babies strung out in a line behind her could keep up with her. As we had no wish to chase and frighten her, we turned the cart round and made our way in the opposite direction.

It was not long before one of the gauchos came galloping up to the cart, his eyes shining, to tell us that not far ahead he could see quite a large flock of rheas crouching in the thistles. He explained that if we went in the cart in a certain direction and I set up the camera, he and the other gauchos would surround the birds and drive them towards me, so that I could film them.

We set off, the cart bouncing and swaying over the tussocks of grass and eventually came to the edge of the huge batch of thistles in which the rheas were hiding. Here I could get a clear and uninterrupted view of the grassland, and it was a suitable place to set up the camera. While I took light readings and got everything ready for the filming, my Argentinian friend had to stand holding a Japanese paper parasol over me and the camera, as the sun was so fierce that a few minutes' exposure to it would make the camera terribly hot, which would ruin the colour film.

When all was ready I gave the signal, and in the distance we could hear the loud whoops of the gauchos as they urged their horses into the prickly thistles, and the scrunch and crackle of the horses' hooves treading the brittle plants underfoot. Suddenly an extra loud chorus of yells warned us that the rheas had jumped up and had started to bolt for it, and within a few seconds five of them crashed out of the thistles and started to run across the grass. They ran as the first one had, with their chins almost touching

their shins and seemed to be travelling as fast as they were able, but I was soon to learn differently. No sooner had the gauchos thundered out on to the turf in pursuit, whirling their boleadoras round their heads with a shrill whistling sound, than all the rheas suddenly seemed to tuck in their bottoms and shoot forward as though they were jet-propelled, nearly doubling their speed within two or three paces. They very soon vanished across the pampas, and the cries of the huntsmen and the beating of the horses' hooves faded into the distance.

I knew that the gauchos would finally catch up

with them, surrounding the birds and driving them back towards me again, and within a quarter of an hour I was once again treated to the sight of the flying rheas speeding across the turf, their feet thumping on the hard ground, while the hunters galloped close behind, uttering shrill cries which mingled with the swishing of the boleadoras. The birds were still running in a bunch, spread out roughly in V-formation.

When they were about a hundred yards away, how-

ever, one of them swerved and started running straight towards the cart where I was standing with the camera. One of the gauchos galloped in pursuit to try to round him up and get him back to the flock. He urged his horse closer and closer to the flying bird, and the closer he got the more worried the rhea became. In fact, he was so concerned with his pursuer that he failed to notice the cart, myself, and the cine-camera. I was looking through the viewfinder and beginning to get a little worried, for he still had not appeared to notice me. It was such a wonderful scene that I did not dare stop filming, but at the same time I had no particular desire to be hit amidships by several hundreds of pounds of rhea, travelling at about twenty miles an hour. At the very last moment, when I felt sure the bird, camera, tripod, and myself were going to go down in a tangled heap in the grass, the rhea caught sight of me. He gave a horrified look at me and twirled round skilfully and dashed off at right angles.

When I measured the distance later, I found that the hunted bird had been within six feet of the camera, but this swerving that he had been forced to do lost him the short lead that he had on the gaucho. The boleadoras whistled and swooped through the air, twined themselves round the rhea's powerful legs and he collapsed in a heap in the grass, flapping and kicking. The gaucho was off his horse in an instant, and rushing forward grabbed the threshing legs. He had to do this very skilfully, and, once having obtained a grip on them, had to hold on tight, for one well-aimed kick of those large feet could quite easily have disembowelled him.

After having examined and obtained close-ups of our catch, we unwound the boleadoras from his neck and legs, and for a few seconds he lay limply in the grass, but then bounded to his feet and trotted off into the thistles in an unhurried manner, joining his companions.

On our way back from the ranch, well pleased with our filming, we came across a rhea's nest: it was just a slight depression in the earth, with ten large bluish-white eggs in it. They were still warm, so the male, who does the work of hatching them out, could only just have left, maybe on hearing our approach, although they are usually very fierce and dangerous during the nesting period.

The gauchos told me that two or three females may use one of these nests in which to lay their eggs, so that you may find anything up to twenty or twenty-five eggs in a nest belonging to several mothers. The father rhea does all the incubating, so all the mothers have to do is to deposit their eggs in the nest and from then onwards father takes over and sits on them until they hatch out, whereupon the mother takes charge of the babies to give them their schooling.

CHAPTER SIXTEEN

In which I have trouble with toads, snakes, and Paraguayans

THE Paraguayan Chaco is a vast, flat plain that stretches from the River Paraguay to the base of the Andes. It is as flat and almost as smooth as a billiard table, and for half the year it is baked dry as a bone by the hot sun, and for the other half it is flooded three or four feet deep in water by the winter rains. As it lies between the tropical forests of Brazil and the grassy pampas lands of Argentina it is an odd country, being a mixture of the two. Here are great grassy fields in which grow palm trees or thorn scrub hung with strange tropical flowers; mixed with the palm trees there are other types of trees not unlike those out of an English wood, except that their branches are covered with long streamers of grey Spanish moss that wave gently in the wind.

We made our base camp in a small township on the banks of the River Paraguay. From here, deep into the interior, ran the Chaco railway; the buckled rails were only some two feet apart and on this rickety and dangerous track ran Ford Eights. By this uncomfortable mode of travel we journeyed quite far inland in search of specimens. The railway line was built on a raised embankment, which was probably one of the only bits of high ground in the territory, and all the animal life would make use of this as a roadway. Travelling along in one of the little cars I could see hundreds of extraordinary birds in the undergrowth along the sides of the track: toucans, with their great clownish bags, jumping and scuttling among the branches of the trees, seriemas, looking like big grey turkeys, strutting across the grass fields; and everywhere beautiful black and white fly-catchers and humming-birds. Sometimes in rounding a corner we would come across some animal on the track. It might be an armadillo, or perhaps an agouti, which looks

like a gigantic reddish-coloured guinea pig; or it might, if you are lucky, be a maned wolf, a huge animal with long slender legs clad in untidy, loose, red-coloured fur.

It was not long after our arrival that we obtained our first specimens. The local people, when they learnt that we were willing to buy animals, used to go out hunting for us, and one of the creatures they were very successful in capturing was the three-banded armadillo, or, as it is known in Spanish, the orange armadillo, from its habit of rolling up into a complete ball roughly orange-shaped. It is in fact the only armadillo which can roll itself up like this and is, moreover, the only one of this family that regularly comes out during the daytime. Trotting about in search of food, which consists of roots and insects, the little creature will curl itself up tightly into a ball and remain quite still if it suspects anything dangerous is approaching, in the hope that its enemy will mistake it for a stone, which, as a matter of fact, it very much resembles. These armadillos, once you catch sight of them, are very easy to capture. The men would ride through the undergrowth until they saw one of these animals and then they would just simply dismount from their horses, pick it up and pop it into a bag.

Now normally members of the armadillo family are very easy to keep in captivity. They are fed on fruit and vegetables and carrion, but these little three-banded armadillos were a very different proposition. They refused, a first, to take any of the food which must have been their natural diet and seemed positively afraid when offered insects. After a lot of experimenting, I got them on to a diet of raw meat mixed with egg and milk, to which vitamins were added. On this they seemed to thrive, but another difficulty soon made itself apparent. The wooden floor of the cage affected their hind feet and very soon the soles became worn so that they were all red and raw. Therefore, everyday the little creatures had to be taken out of the cage and have the soles of their feet treated with penicillin ointment; but the real problem was to find a suitable flooring for them. I tried them on mud, but they just simply plastered this into a sort of cement by slopping their milk on to it and treading it down, and this had much the same effect on their paws as the wooden boards. After a time, I found the ideal bottom surface for them was a thick layer of sawdust. On this they could trot about quite happily without damaging their feet in any way.

Like the Argentinian gauchos, the Paraguayans eat these little animals when they catch them, but unlike the Argentinian armadillo, the hard horny carapace of the three-banded armadillo can be used for a variety of things. Sometimes the shell is rolled up into a ball, fastened with wire and made into a little round

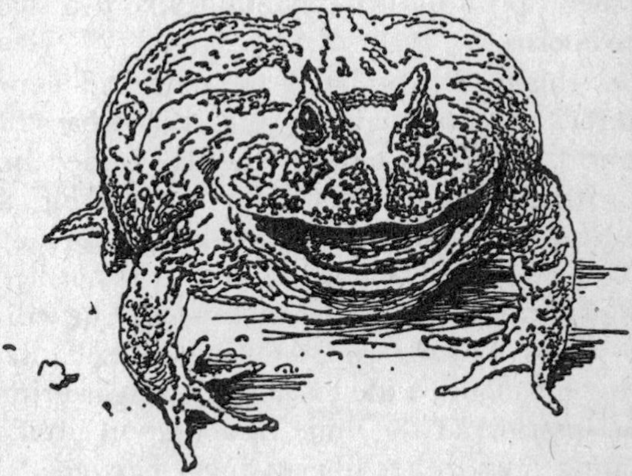

work-basket, and at other times skin is stretched across the hollow inside of the carapace, a handle fixed, and some strings fixed to it, and it is thus made into a small guitar. So the three-banded armadillo is much sought after by the inhabitants of the Chaco, because he is not only good to eat but is useful for other reasons.

Being so flat, large areas of the Chaco are, of course, permanently flooded, and in these swampy districts the most extraordinary forms of reptile and amphibian life are to be found. One of the commonest creatures, and one which all the natives fear, is the horned toad. These weird-looking beasts grow to a very large size. The biggest one we caught would have covered a fair-sized saucer. They are beautifully coloured with bright emerald-green, silver, and black on a cream background. They have what must be one of the largest mouths in the toad world: it is so wide that it looks as though, like Humpty Dumpty, if they grinned they would split themselves in half. Over each eye the skin is hitched up into a little pyramid, like two sharply-pointed horns.

Now, this toad is probably the most bad-tempered and ferocious amphibian not only in the Chaco but in the world. It spends most of the day buried in soft mud with just its horns and its eyes sticking above the surface. If you find one and dig him out, he will become terribly indignant and will not hesitate to attack. Standing on his fat, stumpy legs, he will give little jumps towards you, blowing himself up and opening his mouth wide to show the bright primrose-yellow interior; at the same time he will utter loud screaming yaps, rather like an angry pekinese.

The inhabitants of the Chaco are quite convinced that the horned toad is deadly poisonous. Well, of course, there are no poisonous toads in the world, and so, when I caught my first horned toad, I decided to show the people that they were really quite harmless. I lifted him out of his box and he immediately started struggling in my hand, uttering his loud piercing yaps and opening his mouth wide. As soon as his mouth was open, I pushed one of my fingers into it, in order to show that his bite was harmless. A second or two later, I bitterly regretted my demonstration, for his jaws closed on it, like a vice, and the tiny, but sharp, little teeth in his jaws dug into the flesh. It felt exactly as if my finger had been jammed in a door, and it took me a minute or so before I could prise open his jaws and hurriedly withdraw it, by which time I had a deep red groove right round the finger, which took a day to disappear, and I also had a black mark on my thumb near where his jaws had snapped close. After this I treated the horned toad with more respect when I picked up one.

Another extraordinary amphibian that I caught was called the Budgetts Frog. Now these are very similar to the horned toad to look at, and in fact are related to him. They have the same wide mouth and short, stocky legs, but the bulge over their eyes is round instead of being pointed into horns. They are a dark chocolate-brown on top with whitish-coloured tummies tinged with yellow. Unlike the horned toad, they spend their whole lives in the water, floating spread-eagled on the surface, with their eyes protruding above it. Like their cousins, they are bad-tempered beasts, and when angry will give a yapping shrill cry, very like that of a horned toad only higher and more prolonged. The skin of their bodies is very fine, so that when they blow themselves up in anger it swells like a balloon. The local people say that sometimes these frogs will inflate themselves to such an extent that they will burst, and though I never saw this happen, I believe that it might well be possible.

Of course, where frogs and toads are found in any quantity, snakes, who feed on them, will automatically be found, and the Chaco is no exception to this rule, for here you find very lovely forms of snake life. There is the rattlesnake, for example; the handsome grey and black fer-de-lance, perhaps the most deadly snake in South America; also there are many extraordinary kinds of water and tree snakes, some brightly coloured and others dull.

The poisonous snakes in the world are divided into three groups: the really deadly ones are called the front-fanged snakes, which have their fangs in the front of their mouth, and which are generally large and can inject a considerable quantity of poison; and then there is the group known as the rear-fanged snakes: these have the poison fangs situated to the back of the mouth, and are generally not very long. In the rear-fanged group, the poison is not used so much for defence as for the capturing of their prey, so usually their poison is mild, and sometimes on even such a small animal as a lizard it has only a slightly paralysing effect. However, even if you were bitten by a rear-fanged snake there is a chance that blood-poisoning might set in, so it is an experience which should be avoided.

One of the loveliest snakes we caught was the hooded snake. This reptile looks as though it has been cast in a mould of deep bronze with blackish markings round the edge of the body. It has the curious habit, when angry, of being able to extend the skin of the neck, so that it appears extraordinarily like a hooded cobra in a rage. It is only a mildly poisonous kind of reptile and is one of the rear-fanged group, living on frogs and small rodents, with possibly an occasional bird. The hooded snake does not require a great deal of poison to subdue his prey, and so, though he looks very deadly, his bite, which can be extremely painful, is not fatal.

Perhaps the most beautiful snakes found in the

Chaco are the coral snakes. These are very deadly little reptiles, but by their coloration they warn you in advance of what they can do. They measure perhaps eighteen inches or two feet in length and are banded from head to tail with rings of cream, coal-black, and pink or pillar-box red.

Then, of course, there is the giant anaconda, the huge water-snake that is a relative of the python of Africa, and who catches and crushes his prey in the same way. Now, there have been a great many stories written about them, most of which are entirely untrue. The largest specimen on record is twenty-five feet long, which is not really long as these snakes go, for a Malayan python may grow to thirty feet or over. Like all these giant snakes, the anaconda is not vicious and he will not go out of his way to attack you if you leave him alone. If cornered, however, this reptile might manage to sink his teeth into you and throw a couple of coils around you, and a large specimen could prove a very nasty customer.

In the flooded areas of the Chaco there were quite a number of these anacondas, and one day a local farmer came and told me that the previous night one of them had raided his chicken-run and stolen two chickens. He had followed the trail of crushed grass and weed made by the snake into the swamp behind his farm, and said that he knew the place where the creature was lying up to digest his meal. He went on to say that he would lead me to the spot if I would like to try to catch the reptile. We set off on horseback and circled through the swamp towards the place where he said the snake was resting. In spite of our cautious approach, however, the anaconda caught sight of us before we arrived at the spot and all that could be seen were the ripples as he swam away rapidly through the water. It was impossible to follow fast enough on horseback in that depth of water, so the only thing to do was to follow him on foot. I jumped off the horse, grabbed a sack that we had brought with us, and ran as quickly as I could in the direction that the snake had taken. I found that he was wriggling towards the edge of the swamp, in order to try to escape into the

dense undergrowth there and thus evade us, but he was so bloated with his chicken dinner that he could not travel at any speed, and I caught him up in the short grass at the edge of the bank long before he reached the bushes.

Now, to catch one of these big snakes is very easy: you seize him by the tail, pull him out and then try to get a good grip on the back of his head. This is exactly what I did, and I hauled the angry reptile out of the undergrowth and grabbed him behind the head before he could turn and strike me. He was about nine feet long, and so was quite safe to handle by myself. To cope with anything over that length would have required two people. Once I had a good grip on the back of his neck, I simply held him down in the grass until my companion joined me, when, with his help, I managed to get the wriggling and hissing, and extremely annoyed, anaconda into the bag.

It is necessary when catching a snake of any sort, even one like this anaconda, to examine it as soon as you reach your camp. There are several reasons for this. First, however carefully it is captured, there is a risk that you might break one of the very fragile ribs which snakes possess, and a broken rib can give a great deal of trouble. Secondly, you look for ticks. A snake can be simply covered in ticks and can do very little to get rid of them. They fasten themselves on the thin skin between the scales, sometimes in such numbers that the scales drop off and an ugly bare patch of roughened skin is left, so it is very important to remove the ticks, otherwise the appearance of your snake may be ruined.

Now you just can't pull a tick off. If you do, its mouth parts will be left imbedded beneath the surface of the skin and create a tiny sore which might turn into a nasty ulcer. The best way to remove ticks is with a little paraffin, or failing that, by touching them with a lighted cigarette, whereupon they will loosen their grip and fall off.

Another thing you have to look for is any old wounds that the reptile might have received and which may be in need of attention. When a snake sheds its skin, which occurs regularly throughout the year, it leaves a perfect transparent replica of itself behind, even to the two scales that look like minute watch-glasses that cover its lidless eyes. Occasionally, however, as the creature wriggles through thorn bushes or rocks in an effort to work the skin loose, it will tear, and though the reptile usually gets rid of the whole of the skin it may be left with the two watch-glass scales still covering the eyes. This causes partial blindness, and if the scales are left on for too long, the creature may become permanently blind. So with a newly caught snake you must always examine its eyes to see if the last time it shed its skin its eyes were freed from the two watch-glass scales.

CHAPTER SEVENTEEN

The story of Cai; Pooh; and Sarah Huggersack the only ant-eater film-star

THERE are not a great many kinds of monkey found in Chaco, but while we were there we were fortunate enough to obtain a specimen of one of the rarer ones, and what must be one of the strangest monkeys in the world. It is called the douroucouli and is the only nocturnal monkey known. It has enormous eyes, rather like an owl's, and is coloured silver-grey on its back with a lemon-coloured tummy and chest. During the day, these monkeys sleep in hollow trees, or some other dark place, and as soon as it begins to grow dark they venture out and spend the whole night wandering in large parties through the forest, searching for food, such as fruit, insects, tree frogs, or birds' eggs.

Now, when we first caught Cai, as we called her, she was very thin and miserable-looking, but a few weeks on a good diet with plenty of milk and cod-liver oil soon put her right. Cai was a very charming little animal and though she was very tame, she was extremely nervous, and so you could not treat her in quite the same way as any other sort of monkey. I built her a nice cage, in the top of which was a square bedroom for her sleeping quarters. Cai, being like all monkeys very inquisitive, could not bear not to know all that was going on around her, so during the day she would lie half in and half out of her bedroom door, her head nodding as she dozed, but waking instantly and chirruping with curiosity should anything happen in the camp.

She refused all food except milk, hard-boiled eggs, and bananas, though she would occasionally take a lizard. She seemed, however, to be quite frightened of insects, and when I gave her a tree frog she took it in her hand, smelt it, dropped it with an expression of disgust, and then wiped her hand vigorously on the side of the cage. Towards evening, she would become very lively and be quite ready for a game, bounding up and down in her cage, her big eyes shining and reminding me of the galagos that I had collected in West Africa. She displayed a great deal of jealousy towards the other animals if we took any notice of them, and particularly to a crab-eating racoon, called Pooh.

Pooh was a strange little creature with great big flat paws, and a black mark across his eyes made him look not unlike a giant panda. Pooh always wore a very dismal expression and looked as if everything depressed him, but it was his large hands with their long thin fingers that we had to watch, for he could push them between the bars of his cage and steal anything within reach with the greatest of ease, and he was so curious that he would do his very best to get hold of almost anything. He would lie for hours on his back in the corner of his cage, plucking in a thoughtful sort of way at the hairs on his large tummy. When he grew tame, we could put our hands inside the cage and play with him. He used to love these games, pretending to bite, rolling over and kicking his big paws in the air.

When he grew very tame, we made him a little collar and used to let him out on a very long rope tied to a stick in the middle of the camp clearing. We had another stick farther along, to which Cai, the monkey, was tied. The very first thing in the morning, when Pooh saw the food basket arriving, he would start uttering his loud complaining screams for food, and in sheer desperation we would have to give him some-

thing to keep him quiet. If we did this, Cai would become jealous, and when it came to her turn to be fed she would sulk, turning her back on us and refusing the food.

Strangely enough, Cai was rather afraid of Pooh, though she did not at all mind a pair of baby deer whose little pen was near to her stick, and she would frequently go and lie quite close to the bars while the deer sniffed at her in an astonished sort of manner. Another thing that she was frightened of was snakes. When I brought back the anaconda, whose capture I mentioned in a previous chapter, and took him out of his sack to examine him, Cai, who was sitting in the bottom of her cage, took one look and fled up to her bedroom, much to our amusement, where she sat, peering timidly round the door and uttering horrified twittering noises.

One morning, as we were cleaning out the cages, a young Indian came into the camp and asked if we would like to buy an animal off him. We asked him what sort of an animal it was and he explained that it was a baby fox. We thought it might be interesting to take a look at it, so we told him to bring it along later in the day. As he did not turn up, we thought he had forgotten all about it, and that we wouldn't get our baby fox after all. To our surprise though, just before luncheon the following day, he came into the camp, dragging a small creature behind him. This was our long-promised baby fox. In appearance he was very like an Alsatian puppy, and he was so frightened that he was inclined to snap. We put him into a cage and gave him a plateful of meat and milk, and left him to calm down. We then sat back and watched him very carefully. The thing that seemed to interest Foxey was to see which of our tamer animals that came near to his cage he could get hold of. Although he was bloated with food he was constantly on the look-out for an even tastier dish. We had a number of tame birds at that time which were allowed to wander freely round the camp, but we soon had to alter this as every now and then we would hear squawks and have to rush to the rescue of some bird which had approached too closely to the fox's cage. Later on, as he became tamer, we also had him out on a lead with Pooh and Cai, but with large distances between them.

To our astonishment, he used to act in exactly the same way as a dog, for when we arrived in the morning he would whine excitedly until we went to talk to him, whereupon he would dance round and round our legs and wag his tail vigorously, a most unfox-like thing to do.

Amongst the specimens we brought back to camp from one of our trips were three large green parrots, all very talkative and full of mischief. At first, we put them all in one cage, thinking that they would be perfectly all right together. Almost immediately the three parrots began to fight, and the noise was so great that we were forced to take out the ringleader and put him in a separate cage. We thought this would create a better atmosphere in the camp once more. We had reckoned without one of the other two. He apparently spent all his spare time gnawing frantically at the wire on the front of his cage, and one day there was a terrific burst of chattering and the bird flew off. We made great efforts to capture it, but he was too quick for us and flapped away over the trees, screaming excitedly.

That, we thought, was the end of our parrot. When we got up the following morning, we were amazed to see the parrot back again, sitting on top of his cage, talking to his companion through the wire. When we opened the door, he hurriedly went into the cage again. He had obviously decided that the amount of food he was getting with us made captivity a better proposition than living in the forest.

Shortly before we left Paraguay to return to England, an Indian brought in what turned out to be our most delightful specimen. It was a baby giant ant-eater which could only have been a few days old. We christened her Sarah Huggersack because at that age she would spend all her time clinging to her mother's back, and so when she came to us she wanted to cling on to us all the time, or hug a sack. Sarah had to feel she was holding on to something, and if you put her on the ground she would stagger after you, making loud protesting honking noises, and as soon as you stopped she would scramble up until she was in her favourite position lying across your shoulders. Owing to the fact that she had such long sharp claws and also that she could grip so hard with them, this was a very painful procedure.

We had to feed Sarah on a bottle. She would take four bottles of milk during the day and very soon learnt how to suck from them. While she was drinking, she would allow her long, sticky, snake-like tongue to protrude, so that it dangled down alongside the bottle.

She grew quite rapidly and soon looked upon us as her adopted parents and would have great games with us after taking her food. Sarah liked to be rolled on her back and have her stomach scratched. If you lifted her up and tickled her under the armpits, she would lift both her paws and clasp them over her head, like a boxer who has just won his fight. At other times, if you pulled her tail or tickled her ribs, she would rear up on to her hind legs and fall on you, uttering loud snuffling noises of pleasure.

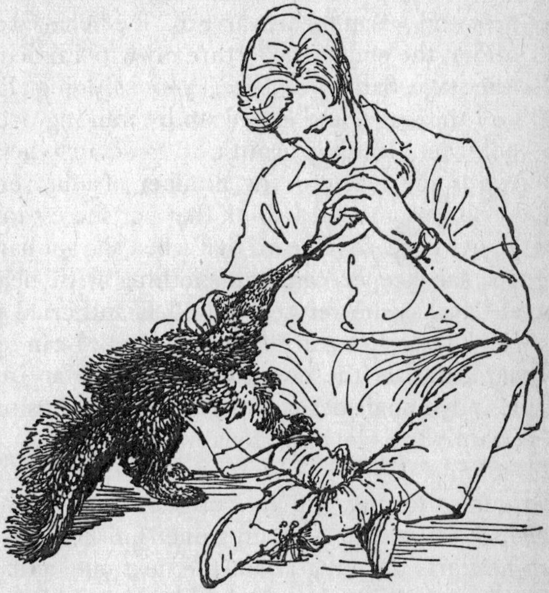

When I eventually arrived back in England, Sarah was one of the first to go with Pooh and Cai to live at Paignton Zoo, where she became a great character. The last time I saw Sarah was a few weeks later. I was giving a lecture at the Festival Hall on animal collecting, and showing the colour film of the trip to Paraguay and Argentina. As Sarah was one of the stars of the film, I wrote to Paignton Zoo and asked if it would be possible for her to come up and appear with me on the stage. The authorities kindly consented to this, and so on the morning of the lecture Sarah Huggersack, accompanied by her keeper, travelled up on the train from Devon.

When she arrived at the Festival Hall she was given a special dressing-room all to herself, which had been kept nice and warm for her arrival. She behaved very well, and at the end of the lecture my wife carried her on to the stage. Sarah was a great success, doing all her tricks on the stage, and ended up by walking over to the table and leaning against it to scratch herself. Afterwards she received any number of admirers in her dressing-room, and I think that her success rather went to her head, for I heard that when she got back to the zoo, the keeper could do nothing with her for several days, as she refused to be left and cried piteously if she was alone in her cage. I think I can safely say that Sarah is the only ant-eater film-star in the world, and though perhaps not as beautiful as some, she certainly has a lot of personality.

So our collecting trip to Paraguay and Argentina ended, but a collector has no sooner finished one trip than he starts thinking about the next one, and, as I write, I am making plans for another expedition. It is always a difficult thing to choose your next collecting ground, for there are so many wonderful places in the world to see and so many extraordinary animals to capture that you generally spend some weeks hesitating before you pick a spot on the map.

One thing a collector knows, however, is that wherever he goes in the world he is sure to meet a great array of fascinating little creatures which are perhaps elusive to capture and difficult to keep. They may cause him much anxiety and sometimes a great deal of trouble, but they will always be interesting and amusing, and when he eventually returns to his own country, he will look upon them not merely as a collection of rare specimens but more like a big family.

INDEX

INDEX

Other Puffin books which you will enjoy are described on the following pages

THE BRUMBY

Mary Elwyn Patchett

The Brumby of this story was a wild Australian stallion, born near the home of a lonely boy, and capturing his imagination with such intensity that he could think and dream of nothing but one day building up a herd of sturdy silver brumbies.

But to the Australian stockmen among whom he lived all brumbies were wild, vicious, untameable animals fit only to be hunted, and young Joey had to endure seeing his beloved foal grow up into a savage outlaw and finally a killer. Nevertheless his dream comes true in the end, although not quite as he'd imagined it.

GREYFRIARS BOBBY

Eleanor Atkinson

The best thing about the story of *Greyfriars Bobby* is that it is absolutely true. There really *was* a little dog in Edinburgh called Bobby: he was a Skye Terrier, and he loved his master, a shepherd called Auld Jock, very dearly. When Auld Jock died Bobby would not leave his grave in Greyfriars Churchyard. People tried to take the little dog away, and found him a home in the country, but still he came back and lived in the churchyard where his friends brought him food. He died after fourteen years and was so famous that a fountain with his statue on it was put up in his memory.

The book includes illustrations taken from Walt Disney's film about him.

TIGER IN THE DARK

Mary Elwyn Patchett

Somewhere in the remote outback, in the centre of the vast continent of Australia, the stories ran, the Queensland tiger still roamed, lurking invisible by day and killing swiftly at night.

This is the story of how a boy and his father set out to find it. Dr Barnett was a distinguished naturalist in search of the truth, and Bruce his son wanted adventure. Together, in the course of a dangerous and exhausting journey, they found both. Bruce's father had warned him of the hardships but they proved even worse than either had imagined – a fight with an infuriated wild stallion is followed by the tortures of thirst which nearly kills them. For readers of 11 and over.

TARKA THE OTTER

Henry Williamson

This story of an otter is as true as long observations and keen insight could make it. It lets you live with Tarka and see at his level (much closer to the ground than our eye level) the wild life of that stretch of Devon country which runs from Dartmouth to the sea, between the rivers Torridge and Taw. With a good map you can follow almost every step of the story.

To read *Tarka* for the first time is a tremendous experience whatever your age. It would be a pity to try it too young, but most people over 10 will enjoy it.

SNOW CLOUD, STALLION

Gerald Raftery

Ken, a young boy working on his uncle's farm in Vermont, first caught sight of Snow Cloud one evening at sundown – a grey stallion, throwing up his head in the mist, galloping away into the shadows. It was no ghost, but a horse which had been badly treated and now ran wild on the mountain. Slowly and patiently Ken began to tame him, first persuading him to take sugar from his hand, learning to ride him, teaching him to come right into the farmyard without being afraid, gradually coaxing him back from his unbroken wildness. Once known as a dangerous animal, Snow Cloud becomes a hero when he helps to bring home a sick man, found lying unconscious in the snow.

THE CUSTER WOLF

Roger Caras

One April five wolf cubs were born in a cave under a tree stump and one was different from the rest. He was white, and men would come to call him by a name that would live in history, for this was the beginning of the legend of the Custer Wolf.

From the moment he was born his life was a struggle, first for milk and then to learn everything he had to know before the cruel winter came. But this wolf inexplicably grew up different from any other, he was a beautiful but solitary animal and as he grew it became clear that he killed for the love of killing and terrorised a huge area round the town of Custer for six whole years. Sometimes he killed thirty cattle in a week, more than he could possibly eat, and he took incredible chances, yet he escaped every trap that was set and every gun that was fired. Small wonder that men believed the white wolf was charmed.